AGAINST THE WIND

DOROTHEE SOELLE

MEMOIR OF A
RADICAL CHRISTIAN

Translated by Barbara and Martin Rumscheidt

Fortress Press ▪ Minneapolis

AGAINST THE WIND
Memoir of a Radical Christian

Cover design: Joseph Bonyata
Author photo: Brigitte Friedrich
Interior design: Julie Odland Smith

Library of Congress Cataloging-in-Publication Data

Sölle, Dorothee.
    [Gegenwind. English]
    Against the wind : memoir of a radical Christian / Dorothee Soelle ; translated by Barbara and Martin Rumscheidt.
        p.   cm.
    Includes bibliographical references (p.   ).
    ISBN 0-8006-3079-3 (alk. paper)
    1. Sölle, Dorothee. 2. Theologians—Germany—Biography.
I. Title.
BX4827.S65A3 1999
230'.044'092—dc21
[B]
                                            99–17388
                                            CIP

The paper used in this publication meets the minimum requirements for American National Standard for Information Sciences—Permanence of Paper for Printed Library Materials, ANSI Z329.48–1984.   ∞™

Manufactured in the U.S.A.   AF 1-3079
03 02 01   00   99   1   2   3   4   5   6   7   8   9   10

Dedicated to my son Martin
the "existentialist"—
that's what a Jewish friend called him as a baby
on account of Martin Heidegger.
In the footsteps of Martin of Tours,
he preferred caring for the aged
to preparing for war.
To the skeptic
who keeps his distance from his third namesake
the great Martin Luther
but not without raising protest
more politely than his mother
more restrained than his sisters
and to this very day more reliably
than all of us.

CONTENTS

A TRIBUTE
BY ROBERT MᶜAFEE BROWN

dorothee soelle
A Lutheran who is also a sectarian
a poet who is also an essayist
a systematic thinker who also lives and writes with passion
a believer in life who can live creatively
        within the reality of death
acquainted with eschatological exuberance
she insists that we pray for the world, but only as
        we strive to live within it
made from dust and created in God's image she gives
        us ground for hope
she believes, along with Dietrich Bonhoeffer, in both
        resistance and submission but only in their
                proper proportions
she fits no conventional categories and can employ a
        fairy tale to make a point
she is a pacifist who can demand stern commitments because
        they are already part of her own life
she is an activist who is also a mystic
she refuses to separate prayer and politics and
        stresses the redemptive possibilities in every
                human situation
as a scholar, she is deeply immersed in the prophets
and as a feminist she is committed to equal rights
        for all God's children everywhere

• • • • •

Join her. It will be worthwhile;
        she presents her faith on her own authority, which she has
        already donated to the glory of God

FOREWORD
BY DANIEL BERRIGAN, S.J.

This is the highest honor I can offer: The life of Dorothee Soelle speaks for itself. It needs no justification; it registers no longing to prove itself, to base an appeal on status, education, gender, color, theological niceties. Indeed the life of Dorothee has been blessed with all the above and more; admiration and friendship come to mind. So does that ironic, unexpected last "blessing" promised the disciples. First, plenty of good things: "homes, brothers and sisters, mothers, children and property." Then the twister: "and persecution besides."

In a sense dear to Bonhoeffer, this woman's theology is worldly. One thinks: as the Incarnation is worldly. From Latin America to the U.S. to Europe she has tested the gospel (and been tested!), laying the Word against the realities of this horrific century—torture, disappearance, oligarchic immunity, enforced misery, weapons, warfare, the buttoned-up arrogance of the great powers.

And in personal life as well, testing, testing—in marriage and motherhood, in being pilloried and denied academic place. In aligning herself, to put the matter briefly, with the plight of Jesus in his century or ours; one and the same.

Her writing, here and elsewhere, has the edge and clarity of a telegram to the world. One does not waste words; the time is short. Speak up then, shout aloud, on behalf of the inarticulate and victimized.

And remember, an intellectual also has a heart.

Therefore this heartfelt book. Which is as much about friendship as anything else—or more so.

Let me rejoice, too, in a long friendship with Dorothee. I learn from her. Theology must not be mired or stalemated in the mind. It must enable, induce an imperative.

Stand squarely in the world. And once there, withstand.

PREFACE

Afew years ago, my friend and editor Johannes Thiele suggested that I write an autobiography. "Are you crazy? I am no unharnessed politician, and I have better things to do!" was my first reaction. But he did not let go. And so a productive tussle arose about what was important and worth telling, what was already prefigured or hinted at in various places of my books and talks, and what could be taken over, brought together, and left out. The result of that tussle or pleasant *cooperatio* is before you. *Thank you,* dear Johannes. Every headwind also has its upward draft.

Much is missing that a classic autobiography would contain. I have told nothing about my father, nothing about the encounters with Hannah Arendt, Ernst Bloch, President Gustav and Ms. Hilda Heinemann, Premier Johannes Rau. Nor is there anything about my abhorrence of crocheting and knitting or enough about my favorite activities, swimming and singing. I have preferred to speak about certain central aspects of life in poetry, seeing that life brings along enough prose as it is.

I am very glad that this book now also appears in English. It is surely no coincidence that a German woman-theologian, who has become rather well-known, found no teaching position in her fatherland but could work in the more liberal world of the American academy. The encounter with that world has enriched and formed me to an extraordinary degree: Being "right in the belly of the beast," as we used to say, that world deepened my fears, but much more than that, it strengthened my hope in people who do not submit to the dictates of the economy, the military, and the advertising industry. Indeed, there was and still is what we always called the "other America."

It is in this sense, then, that I thank all those who had a part in the publication of this book, especially Barbara and Martin Rumscheidt, my translators, with whom I spent many hours in pleasant conversation about a turn of phrase or a title or something that could be left out. I also want to thank Marilyn Legge who read the English text; at an earlier time, she was—with Karen Bloomquist and Christine Gudorf—my best teaching assistant while I was in New York.

This has brought me now to a sort of supplementary dedication that I want to provide for the journey of this English-language edition. I dedicate this book to

- my American alma mater, Union Theological Seminary in New York,

- all my colleagues who gave me the gifts of consideration with a smile, patience, practical advice, and critical head-shakes, but above all their friendship,

- the former and the current presidents of the Seminary,

- the students from every corner of the world who then expanded my vision and even now fashion a better connection between theology and piety than that which came into being in Europe, and

- above all, the many who made that school of learning into a place of common life, in the offices and apartments, in the kindergarten and the quad, in the dining hall, and, not least, the chapel.

Written on the walls of a public building in Manhattan, I saw these words one day: Enlightenment, Faith, Vision. This combination is not altogether well-known in Europe, but it fascinated me. I wish all my American readers a full measure of those three great traditions. They converge with one of my basic experiences: that every headwind does indeed have its upward draft.

LITTLE MATCH-STICK

I t must have been my first year of school, when I was five and a half and undeniably small. I recall my father's words, "The child's not growing, the child's not growing!" My female teacher called me "little match-stick." During the latter part of my half-hour trip home from school, I usually had to walk alone. It was here on Marienburger Street, a boulevard in the south end of Cologne, that a dog came racing toward me. He seemed huge and utterly unstoppable; I was certain he would seize and devour me. My deciding not to try to get out of his way is a moment I remember vividly. I recall the same cold fearlessness in the midst of fear that I experienced later in air-raid shelters during the bombing attacks. It is a kind of fatalism that comes from seeing how great the danger really is.

The dog bowled me over and galloped on. When I reached home, I was crying because of shame, not pain. My three older brothers poked fun at me, wondering whether the dog, in "running me over," had dropped something on me. I protested that it was bigger than any dog I knew, more like a calf. They all laughed at that.

I knew that from every conceivable perspective it was advantageous to be a boy. Something prevented most women from ever becoming what in our childhood games we called "an Indian"; they always remained "palefaces." My mother said that men are better off, except for one thing: they can't have children. I did not find having children as important as going to sea or hacking one's way through the jungle and living in a tree house.

When I was twelve, I practiced swinging on a framework made for carpet-beating. One day, I suddenly saw—no, I distinctly noticed—that I was getting a bosom. Where previously everything had been flat, now there was a tiny swelling. This came as a shock to me. Until then I had believed that one day a piece of bone in my joints would just expand, and at once I would be bigger and stronger. But those budding breasts pre-empted such fanciful dreams. There was to be no transversion; I was born

1

destined to be a girl. Later I read in Sigmund Freud that anatomy is fate—a sentence from the perspective of those unaffected, those who dominate. Never again would I go swinging on that crossbar. I can remember myself having just turned fourteen in the fall of 1943. I was in a Cologne streetcar, staring at a girl with large black eyes. She was standing near me at the back of the car, her hair in a thick brown braid. To me, a skinny waif with bobbed blond hair, she looked wonderful, mysterious, and sad. I desperately tried to find a way to speak to her. Our eyes met, and I imagined that a little smile crossed her face. Then, at the next stop, some soldiers—or were they policemen?—appeared at the front of the streetcar. My girl kept glancing around again and again, and then moved suddenly to get off. As she stepped down, the case she held clutched to her chest shifted, exposing a yellow patch. On it was written the word "Jew," in black letters. I wanted to jump off the streetcar and pursue her, but we were already moving on through the November rain.

On that occasion, I discovered my own cowardice in a personal and political dimension. As the Number 11 made its way through the Severin district of Cologne that day, I remember noting with horror what was in me. Who *am* I if I cannot even get off a streetcar and catch up with an anonymous human being who touches my heart?

A classmate of my brother asked whether his mother could stay with us for a time. She was Jewish; her marriage to an "Aryan" had initially protected her, but now she faced the threat of deportation. For about six weeks this woman was in my parents' home; she lived in the guest room on the top floor, where she was locked in and had to keep completely still when the cleaning lady came.

I became friends with Ms. B., visiting her often in her room under the roof. In those days, when there was an air raid, we used to go to a somewhat more secure basement shelter across the street. Of course, we could not take her with us, so we worried that we would come back and find her wounded or buried in rubble. One day I expressed my concern about what might happen to her. "Don't think about it," she said. "They won't get me." She reached for her ever-ready purse, opened it, took out something and placed it in my hand. It was a small vial; how cold it felt to me. "They won't get me," she said. "Do you understand?" It was poison, and today I can still feel how cold the glass was on my palm. On that day, I stopped being a child.

In those years, from 1943 to 1946, I lived in what is a natural state of opposition to my parents, and to my oldest brother, whose understanding

of the political situation was very clear. We younger ones wanted to separate ourselves from adults who complained about how hard it was to get
enough to eat, from the inconsequential matters that preoccupied our
teachers, and from the utter senselessness of the hours and hours spent in
air-raid shelters during our school days in Cologne. We dismissed all that
as *spiessig*, philistine. Instead, we recaptured moments of Germany's
Jugendbewegung (a youth movement of the first third of the twentieth century, critical of much of Western culture); we sang whatever we could get
our hands on: European folk tunes that had been left out of our song-
books, chorales, and the like.

This was the world of my diaries, an enchanted world of reverie that
featured prominently the adjectives "divine," "unparalleled," and
"immense." Mine was a very apolitical world, if one disregards the preoccupation with the mythic "Germany." It took me a long time to demystify
the allure of the idea that "Germany is borne in the heart, and never anywhere else." The end of the war served to reinforce that tragic myth rather
than unmask it.

From the end of 1944 onward, we experienced hunger; it occupies a
central place in my memory. I lay in bed and thought of spaghetti. We
went to the country and gathered pears. I tried to get out of these foraging
trips after it became obvious to me that as a family, we had no exchange
goods. Even before the house of my parents was fire-bombed at the end of
1944, we could not procure food with volumes of classics or piano edi-
tions of operas. And in the worn-out overcoats of my brothers, I froze.

In autumn of 1945, the schools opened again; with chilblained legs I
waited many hours for the streetcar. One day I just managed to get my
foot on the step and cling to the side of the car, which was against the
rules. I was apprehended, and I had to report with my father to a military-
style court. We got away with a warning, but what amazed me most was
that my father, a lawyer by profession, did not admonish me. He took me
to task instead for my political convictions, asking me once during lunch
whether I seriously intended to defend the Nazis. What I sensed at the
time, but could not even concede to myself, was that my father had the
truth on his side.

I tried to make a distinction between Germany, the dream, and the
Nazis, whom, almost without exception, I found repugnant or trivial. As a
child, I had heard Thomas Mann speaking to us from his exile in Califor-
nia. At the beginning of the war, my parents had bought what was then
called a "people's receiver," a radio. We tuned in to Radio Beromünster

from Switzerland, and, before Holland was occupied, to Hilversum Two. My parents had many Jewish friends, and by the time I was eight or nine, I had known what a concentration camp was. As children of parents opposed to the Nazis, we literally grew up with two languages. At home, there was plain language that named the shootings, torture, and deportations. But for school, where frankness was mortally dangerous, our speech was guarded. "Be quiet, or else you'll wind up in a concentration camp," was a household warning. Oddly enough, I did not lose the feeling of living in two languages, even after the war.

I knew much, but certainly not everything: I definitely knew nothing of Auschwitz. But I did know, for example, that the house in Darmstadt, where my grandmother lived, belonged to a Jewish couple. The woman who held the leases was very friendly to us children and we were fond of her. One day when we came for another visit, she was gone. I wanted to know where she was, and the answer was clear enough: "She has been taken to a camp; she sent a postcard saying that, under the circumstances, she was quite well." My grandmother sent a response to Theresienstadt (Terezin); the letter was returned with the postmark "Addressee Deceased." I must have been twelve or thirteen at the time.

THE DIARY OF AN ADOLESCENT

The end of my childhood is something marked very precisely by a feeling of being suddenly alone, as if driven from paradise. It was an evening in spring 1943 that is pasrticularly memorable. I sat down and wrote a poem about the cherry tree in bloom. That little tree in the garden outside my window had told me of something new, unheard of—bliss and pain in one. But at that time, I would never have called it "becoming an adult." I experienced the loss of my childhood with enormous pain. After all, being a child was all I had known. For me, puberty was a fear-filled break-in. Why should I have to leave behind the land where there was no fear—my childhood? Suddenly I was expelled from the world of trust, of play and imagination. I had loved playing with dolls, but I did not take them to bed with me or dress them up. Instead, I took them on endless military expeditions and adventurous voyages, as I composed whole novels about them in my head.

Now I felt as if I had been cast adrift, utterly lost in the world. I feared very much for my life at that time, but otherwise I was quite fearless, as young people often are. I found it ludicrous when people in the shelters became scared What was very real to me was the fear of not finding the meaning of life, or of somehow ruining my life, of being merely half instead of whole.

Perhaps it was not until I was twenty-seven years old and had a child that I became an adult, rooted in life. I have no name for the long interval that came before—this time of searching, waiting, and wandering. And did I wander! I went hiking, joined many walking tours, and traveled a lot. It was the unsettledness of youth and the romanticism of the formative years.

Confronted by memories of childhood, of a youth both missed and unredeemed between 1945 and 1949, I recently rummaged through one of my old diaries. Something curious happened: I found that my recollections of the tastes and smells of those years and my record of a young girl's search for herself simply do not match. The events, facts, incidents, and experiences that I remember most vividly do not appear in that utterly inward-focused diary. There I read much about flowers in bloom, thunderstorms over the Rhine, and Beethoven's violin concerto, but nothing about the nights when the bombs fell, the sight of the city in flames, the long lines at the grocery stores, the struggles to get coal.

Pages upon pages of my Gothic scribble tell about the great unhappy, and sometimes happy, loves of a "daughter from a good home," of her love for a female teacher, older female friends, and of her first moves toward boys and young men. Discoveries of the mind, Beethoven's Pathétique and Bach's St. Matthew Passion, of Rilke's *Book of Hours* and Goethe's *The Sorrows of Young Werther* are celebrated there, while the political reality of everyday life enters only at the margins.

I am perplexed by this two-tracked recollection and wonder about the meaning of this web of friendship, feelings, literature, and music in which my friends and I lived and moved. Was it a flight from reality? Or protection against it? Was it a "Consolation of the World," as one of my favorite poems was called? Who would I be without those years of excessive romanticism? To what extent did that romanticism insulate me and create a safe place for me to grow up? To what degree did it seduce me into holding on to and refining, in a sophisticated fashion, the lies that were handed to me?

If there was such a thing as an "inner emigration" from Nazi Germany, surely it was the young people who had the greatest reason or a natural right to do it. To distance oneself and not to become involved was not merely a luxury of the bourgeoisie. It was necessary if one was to dream of another land, a different tomorrow.

And so I find things in my diary that cause me to be both ashamed and amused. For the first time in my life, I had fallen head over heels in love with a female teacher; one of the other girls and I just worshiped her. When she was transferred to another school, I was in utter misery. Eventually, the infatuation grew into a friendship. This woman helped me very much; being with her gave me my first feelings of being an adult. She herself was in love with a married man who took his own life in 1945. When she told me about it—I was only fifteen then—I saw her openness as a huge demonstration of trust, for no one had ever taken me this seriously. There is an entry in my diary about a visit to the dearly beloved teacher and later friend, Germaine:

Cologne, June 19, 1944
It was late when I arrived; we listened first to a cello sonata by Beethoven
(op.102) with a wonderful second movement. She was darning socks while we
listened. I wanted very much to help her but she refused me (the "dummy"!).
While I was preparing a pot of coffee, she tried to get some milk. When she
returned she asked me what my parents had to say about the current political
happenings [the invasion in Normandy and Germany's retaliation with the V-
rockets]. I told her that I never speak to them about this, since they had such
crazy ideas. They absolutely want the war to be lost. She was only a bit aston-
ished and asked what my brothers thought. I replied that Thomas and Otto do
not want us to lose; Carl was more materialistic and philistine. I recall now the
beautiful thing she then said (still darning those socks). She said how glad she
was about the retaliation, for "one sees that the German people are not yet ready
to go under." A moment later, as if talking to the sock, she added: "You, too, are
not yet ready to go under."

My diary makes no mention of my school principal in Jena, who every
Monday in the spring of 1945 made a speech at a school assembly. "Where
there is danger, that which saves also grows," he would say, or, "Stand on
your misery, it will lift you higher." He was quoting Hölderlin, and I
became unsure: Was this *my* Hölderlin? Before the Americans came, he
took his life.

Jena, May 3, 1945
The great war draws to a close. At the head of the troops left in Berlin and fight-
ing against Bolshevism, the Führer has fallen. Nearly all army units have
already surrendered.
I try not to think of it. I read and study Hölderlin, Shakespeare, and Sophocles.
I shall forge myself an armor. Tomorrow I shall make use of it.

Already in 1944, while we were still in Cologne, we had expected the
Americans to march into Germany. They were only thirty kilometers
away, and we could hear the artillery. We were always waiting for liberation. And then we had to flee to Thuringia, where the Americans caught
up with us. Eventually, Thuringia passed into Russian control, but I was
able to get away, with my brother Thomas, before that. My feeling was,
this is a total disaster, we shall never be able to go to school again.
Thoughts raced through my mind: The Morgenthau plan proposes that

Germany's population will be reduced to just half its size, industry will be demolished, there will no longer be any need for the intelligentsia. The "denazification" process did nothing to advance my political formation. It was an arbitrary procedure of the victors, who had no understanding of what the situation under Adolf Hitler was really like.

All Saints' Day, November 1, 1945
Germaine had to present herself to the school board and later again to the British authorities. It would be terrible were she not allowed to teach any more just because she had joined the party and the Nazi girls' organization. Everything she worked and fought for all these decades is now up to the whims of an Englishman! How bitter! R. said the other day that she has not really come to grips with the fact that we have lost the war. This is true for me, too. I am not clear at all about its final consequence. Nearly every day I struggle with this thought. For months (since the capitulation) I have written down nothing political. I simply cannot do it: it takes too much energy.

Germaine was hired to teach in October 1945 after the verdict: "May be employed." The following June she was dismissed for being too "naziistic."

Good Friday, April 19, 1946
She spoke once about politics and said that the news of the concentration camps had utterly shaken her; she also felt guilty. She was always so idealistic. I cannot quite understand her on this matter, perhaps because I personally have no guilt feelings since I am too young.

This discussion did not come up in our classrooms, nor later at university. No one explained the history of modern Germany to us and pointed out which traditions, tendencies, and instincts the Nazis were able to connect with. No one addressed the deep, dark feelings of impotence in the face of those who had more weapons and bombs, and the injured pride of the alleged victims, who really were the first and foremost perpetrators.

Cologne, September 23, 1945
[The writer] Ernst Wiechert spoke to Germany's youth on the radio. We are all very sad, for he said things that didn't reach us in depth, things without color and that fade out.

I wrote Ernst Wiechert months later; the letter took its place alongside all the intense subjectivisms in my diary.

Cologne, April 8, 1946

. . . Are they who believed really guilty? Did you not once say yourself that remorse is not reduced in its essence when it is in relation to something imperfect? Is it not correct and natural, especially for youth, to believe where others are skeptical; to venerate when others condemn, to sacrifice themselves where others see through it all with their clever eyes? I was not one of them; I saw, I knew. I did not believe the phrases; I believed in Germany. And that is the reason why I am so sad: There is nothing in your words about Germany.

I received no reply, and I repressed this document until I reread it this time. It is more than embarrassing; it is a sixteen-year-old human being trying to deal with the sense of a catastrophe, namely the destruction of national identity. Today when I read it I am horrified at such blindness. All the good and decent Germans who "surely believed in humanness, truth, justice, and love"—as I wrote—were caught up in that dream: A terrible fate had befallen us all, we who loved Beethoven and Bach! The injustice done to us: the expulsion from the East, the prisoners of war held and used as slave laborers, the demolition of our industry. All of us, in our anguish cried out to heaven while we flatly denied the far greater injustice we had done to the other peoples of Europe.

There was no consciousness of "who sows the wind shall reap the whirlwind," no admission of the crimes of that mythic "Germany," which I—so obstinate—desperately adjured, no remorse, no sign of atonement, no turning back. Today I ask myself which institutions, groups, or social powers could have initiated such a turning back. Why was the church so silent? Would a young person like me, living in the then-Russian Occupation Zone, have been able to write a letter like that? Would they not have heard something else in addition to perplexity and mourning? And in this miserable aroma of the tragic demise of a grand undertaking, would they not have smelled a rat more quickly?

My shame is greatest when I read an entry that perhaps reveals most clearly how profound the damage was, even in someone who, like me, was privileged in many respects.

November 1, 1945

I discovered the other day, by accident, that Daddy is one-quarter Jewish and was subject to political persecution. At first I was horrified and had feelings of inferiority. I am too "Nazi-infected" and behold the impure and inferior in what is non-Aryan. Very often I wonder—for example when Germaine is so kind to me—what if she knew this? Surely she would be very disappointed. Ah, this is nonsense! She would pay no heed to it. After all, it is only one-eighth!

The last sentence of that helpless sixteen-year-old girl that I must have been is the most disgusting. However open the conversational sphere in my parents' house was in relation to things political and sexual, our parents had still kept this fact from us five children. Only my mother occasionally made the playful remark: "So, what would it mean if you had a Jewish grandmother?" Indeed, this negative feeling did turn into a kind of pride later on. I have relearned thoroughly.

SUSPENDED IN NOTHINGNESS

Two other essential dynamics moved in the spirit's exploration of the teenager that I was: existential philosophy and Christianity. Even as the war drew to its close, my brother Thomas told me of a philosopher who described existence as "thrownness" or being thrown. I was completely taken by one of Martin Heidegger's sentences: "Existence is being suspended in nothingness." I wrote it down and sought sustenance in the scrap of paper that lay on my desk for many years.

New Year's Eve, 1946
This year comes to a close, but I neither know nor expect consolation or help from what is to come. We have not yet reached the utter depths of the abyss. Buried in my books, the poet Kleist, and the history of the Greeks, I look up sometimes and listen: the prisoners of war are not permitted to return, the region of the Saar is no longer German, the demolition of industry continues. I continue on my road, without hope, with little faith, a little tired. All that remains for good is the command to keep one's bearing; every bit of courage is needed in our "thrownness."

In the spring of 1948, I heard an address about Jean-Paul Sartre that fascinated me. I sensed a way out of the Heideggerian blind alley in Sartre's distinction between *en soi* (in itself) that rests in itself and a *pour soi* (for itself) that pushes beyond itself.

March 1948
How everything changes daily! "Behold, I make all things new!" On my table, a Greek New Testament lies next to Sartre's "The Flies." What is the uncanny, the terrific, the lofty and the lowly, the imposing, the great? Lore and I are listening to an address on Sartre. "Freedom has struck me like a stroke of lightening. I am my freedom." Nothing else has become simpler as a result, but more comprehensible and clear.

11

The rubble in my city, Cologne, had not yet been removed; nor is it gone from my inner landscape of the spirit Germany, the winter fairy tale. Yet the ideas that blew over from the other side of the Rhine did strike me like bolts of lightning: Slowly, the nihilism that had been so proud of its depth and irreconcilability lifted.

In retrospect, the time from 1945 to 1949, when I matriculated, looks to me like a darkness that had no beginning. No one helped me understand that the German catastrophe was Germany's liberation. In that downfall, what collapsed was not only the Third Reich but also the world that could not prevent or put a stop to it, the world of the German bourgeoisie. It became more and more difficult for me to reconnect with the liberal bourgeois world in which my parents lived before 1933.

My relationship to Christianity was a critical-liberal one; it had been damaged by the Nazis in a manner completely unknown to me. I respected the church inasmuch as it had dared to speak out now and then against what was happening. I could not call it "resistance" because that was too big a word for the church's actions. I also had not yet come to know Dietrich Bonhoffer and his resistance to the Nazis on the basis of faith. In terms of its substance, however, I viewed faith as an impermissible escape from the darkness that must be borne: Christians were cowards, unable to look nihilism in the eye. I harbored a vulgarized Nietzschean disdain for Christianity.

On the eve of my eighteenth birthday (1947)
B. sits at the piano and plays the Adagio *of the* Pathétique. *Again and again he points the way, provides direction, creates space. But he is a Christian; he backs off at some point, turns pale. Sometimes I am so very lonely. I wish that the human being would come who is all these in one.*

My encounter with Catholic reactionism did the rest. This was the triumphant Catholic blockheadedness that was ensconced in the Rhine region and made itself at home in the girls' school I attended. Our religion classes were so unbearable that my best friends in the grade above mine walked out en masse. I could not bring myself to join in their boycott, because I still wanted to know more—particularly about Jesus, the tortured one who did not become a nihilist.

But my arrogance prevailed; I really could not accept that one had to believe in the Virgin Birth in order to understand the Sermon on the Mount. Soon a new religion teacher made her appearance in my diary. She read Heidegger with us and steered us into a radically different under-standing of Christianity. As for me, I set out to search for my soul in the land of the Greeks. But in my studies I found nothing more than what bourgeois philology had to offer, and that was too little to live on. The nihilism of the recent years had left me hungry. Awakening from the crisis of the liberal bour-geois world of my parents and its Christianity, I finally began to look for another philosophy of life. I studied theology in order to get at the truth that had been kept from me long enough. Slowly, a radical Christianity began to nest in me.

Existential nihilism is a nice place to visit, but you wouldn't want to live there. Some erased it from their minds, or made a new home in the affluent society emerging in the early fifties; little did it matter to them that this affluence was subsidized by the remilitarization of our country. The time for remorse or turning back was slipping away. I tried to make "the leap," as Søren Kierkegaard called it, into the passion for the uncondi-tional, into the reign of God. I began to become a Christian.

WAKING UP

I was born the same year as Anne Frank, 1929. I was twenty years old when I read her diary. In 1950, when the first German edition was published, she had already been dead for more than five years. But the dead do not age; at most, they pale, something unimaginable in relation to Anne. I read her entries as if I had been there in that house in Amsterdam, overlooking the canals. For me, Anne was the friend for whom I had searched so long: witty, curious, intelligent, full of ideas, full of life. Anne would grimace sarcastically over the adults wailing for the china they had to leave behind. Anne was unremitting in her disdain for mediocrity and stupidity. Anne, with the eyes the whole world knows from the photograph, full of sadness but not weepy.

I think that many girls from protected families with high educational expectations devoured this book as I did, as a book for girls, an honest book about the fears and despairs of youth. At the time, the word "puberty" was unknown to me, even though I had suffered through it, and I could not yet distance myself from its loneliness. Anne had written exactly what I too had experienced:

January 30, 1943
Everyone thinks I'm showing off when I talk, ridiculous when I'm silent, insolent when I answer, cunning when I have a good idea, lazy when I'm tired, selfish when I eat one bite more than I should, stupid, cowardly, calculating, etc., etc. All day long I hear nothing but what an exasperating child I am, and although I laugh it off and pretend not to mind, I do mind.

Were not my experiences similar? As a child, I had had to hold my own against three older brothers; I was always "the little one," the little "know-nothing." Whenever I wanted to add to a conversation, I had to produce rational arguments. Anne wrote about the dreadful loneliness of adolescence, and I understood in my heart exactly what she meant.

And yet the sentiments that first drew me to identify with Anne represent only one small part of her; she also demonstrated a genuinely interior, substantive seriousness and incorruptibility. This other voice of Anne speaks precisely where we today, living in a culture dominated by individualistic psychology, would not even listen for it, namely, in her grasp of the inescapable brutality of the world around her. The diary of Anne Frank is the exemplary story of one of the victims of war; it reveals the meaning of "going underground" and the ways in which people tried to avoid persecution. My experiences with the minor evacuations the war caused, such as those that account for my knowing so many schools, always being "the new kid" in class, could never compare.

Anne thought, felt, breathed, and hoped against everydayness and against fear. Not only each day she lived but also each sentence that this girl wrote is stolen from the murderers and given back to life. Therein lies a commandment to all, one that transcends the time of German fascism half a century ago: Wherever human beings are persecuted, carried off, murdered, and disposed of, the voice of Anne Frank is present. It is the voice of one who is half child and half young woman and who challenges the authority of the civil servants of murder.

It is something special to experience Anne Frank from the perspective of a German. The machinery of death to which she was delivered is one that my people conceived, planned, built, oiled, and serviced right to the bitter end. One of the passages I had underlined in my tattered copy of her diary is the following:

> Fine specimens of humanity, those Germans, and to think that I'm actually one of them! No, that's not true, Hitler took away our nationality long ago. And besides, there are no greater enemies on earth than *these* Germans and the Jews. (October 9, 1942)

How often I wished that Hitler had also made me "stateless"! That I did not belong to the people I belong to! Anne Frank's distinction between "these" Germans and others gives evidence of her ability to differentiate, to express herself with precision. But for me, a German, it is not quite so simple. In the end, all who did not put up resistance were implicated, entangled in the belief systems of "these" Germans, lending them a hand and sharing in the profits. Among those who "went along," in the broadest sense of the words, were all who had practiced the art of looking away, turning a deaf ear, and keeping silent. There has been much quarreling about collective guilt and responsibility, but my basic feeling is, rather, one of an ineradicable shame—the shame of belonging to this people, speaking the language of the concentration camp guards, singing the songs that were also sung in the Hitler Youth and the Company of German Girls. That shame does not become superannuated; it must stay alive.

I came to understand this shame after the war, when I visited Anne Frank's host country, the Netherlands, for the first time. There I met people who did not want to speak German. A passerby turned away when I asked her in German for directions. She could see that I was too young to have had an active part in a Nazi organization, but that was irrelevant to her. Shame was within us, and shame was placed upon us from without.

For ten years of my young adulthood I was preoccupied with the questions of my generation: How could this happen? What did my parents do to stop it? What side were my teachers on? Which of my country's traditions had conditioned "it," the only name that we could use for the horror? Did Martin Luther play a part? Richard Wagner? Friedrich Nietzsche? Martin Heidegger? Were our schools not like the barracks? Were families not meant to produce underlings? "Where were you when 'it' happened?" we used to ask the adults. For years, we really did nothing else but ask these questions. Like Oskar, the drummer boy in Günter Grass's *Tin Drum,* who did not want to grow up into someone like the "grownups" around him, we asked ourselves: Who would wish to grow up and belong to the bureaucratic "desk job" perpetrators—the murderers, informers, torturers, railroad workers, or nurses who were involved?

The worst answer to our many questions was the denial of reality. It went more or less as follows: "But we knew nothing about that. We had no contact with Jews. In our village, there was 'no such thing.' One heard awful things about concentration camps, but they were only for criminals and homosexuals, weren't they? And, yes, for Jews." This answer, repeated in a thousand places, only made the shame more inescapable. Sometimes I would counter helplessly: "Have you read *The Diary of Anne Frank?*"

All during the fifties, I wanted to know exactly when, where, how, and by whom Jews had been murdered. Then, in the mid-sixties, I tried to develop a "post-Auschwitz" theology—I did not want to write one sentence in which the awareness of that greatest catastrophe of my people was not made explicit.

How did I come to this position? Nothing I gained in terms of political enlightenment, nothing that slowly brought me out of the murky haze of a tragic, irrational Germanness, came from institutions like the church, school, or political parties. I learned from my parents, eyewitnesses, returning émigrés, refugees, and survivors. I read Eugen Kogon's *The Theory and Practice of Hell* soon after it appeared, and, gradually, the fog of my German, romantic, bourgeois-educated youth began to lift. In other words, it was relatively late that I began the work of dealing with this matter; as it turned out, it became a lifelong process, born from my deep sense of shame.

Collective shame is the minimum required for a people with a history like that of the Germans. But in this shame there is also an element that propels one forward and brings about positive change. A great German philosopher said that shame is "a revolutionary virtue." I really believe that shame has made some changes in my people. There was a slogan used in the early days of the peace movement of the '80s (and only in Germany could it have been phrased like this): "This time no one can say, 'We did not know.'" This message was carried around on placards and painted on walls. Among us, there was so much that was understood ever so late and always by the minority: Arming ourselves will be followed by war; greater power to the police heightens the possibility of state terrorism; baiting and defaming other races and groups conditions readiness to persecute them.

Today, when I meet someone of my generation and level of education who does not know what Cyclon B is, I become nervous. And I am ashamed again, anew: by the poison gas that German industrialists sold to Israel's enemies or by the billions German Marks that we could spare for the Gulf War but not for providing potable water to countries plagued with cholera. I need this shame about my people; I do not want to forget anything, because forgetting nurtures the illusion that it is possible to be a truly human being without the lessons of the dead. The truth of the matter is that we need their help. I needed my friend Anne Frank very much.

CHOOSING ONE'S TEACHERS . . .

I must confess that, owing to the insulation my parents' home provided, my awareness of reality had been limited. I assumed that if you wished to know the truth, as I did, you went to college. By studying literature, theology, and philosophy, I thought, I might perhaps get a job teaching. The idea of becoming a minister never crossed my mind. I took innumerable detours along the way. At the theological faculty, we women found ourselves in the minority and, academically, mostly in the above-average group.

Already in the last years of high school, helped by my religion teacher, I had become fascinated by a non-churchy, radical Christianity. The classes of Marie Veit, my teacher, were fantastic and electrifying. Today I am amused by my diary account of those days: "The new religion teacher is overwhelmingly good but—alas!—she's Christian." What stands out here is an eighteen-year-old's arrogance and her notion that Christians are just dumb, backward, cowardly, and obtuse. It would take some time for me to concede that whatever was fascinating me was much stronger than my own wisdom. On the intellectual road to Athens, I suddenly realized that right from the start, Jerusalem was where I really wanted to go!

Marie Veit is one of the most critical and constructive women theologians in the German-speaking world. Even before the emergence of the term in the Latin-American context, she was a "liberation theologian," articulating the need for another Christianity after the experience of German fascism. But being a woman of her generation (and my own), in the Federal Republic of Germany, precluded pursuing the career she deserved. Woman-specific impediments both delayed her entry to university teaching and inhibited her readiness to commit things to print.

In 1947, only a few years older than we, she entered our eleventh-grade classroom in the Cologne high school for girls. She was an utterly incorruptible and exacting teacher who both demanded and exemplified intellectual rigor and candor, like her teach Rudolf Bultmann, who had

CHOOSING ONE'S TEACHERS . . .

directed her doctorate. Marie Veit had an inimitable way of subverting my annoyance with Christianity. In response to my offensives against fawning humility, or pious murmurings about the beyond, she would ask politely whether it was Paul, or Martin Luther, or the Gospels I had in mind. She was a marvelous teacher who never prohibited my cheekiness and bold comments but always required that I be clear. Today I think that she respected my anger and was bemused by my arrogance. Challenging our intelligence, she simply trusted people's capacity for comprehension and conscience.

Freezing cold and grateful for school lunches, we studied Martin Heidegger and Jean-Paul Sartre, Dietrich Bonhoeffer and Paul, and, after school, Herbert Marcuse and Sigmund Freud. Years later in Cologne, the Ecumenical Working Group was founded and developed into the "Political Evensong." With her expertise, theological knowledge, organizational initiative, and talent, Marie Veit was a "pillar" of that group in word and deed. I remember her matchless ability to help older members of the congregation distinguish between Christian faith and bourgeois respectability.

The intervening decades have deepened and tested Marie Veit's engagement in the great confrontations between the rich and the poor, between those who live without weapons and those who profit from the arms industry, between biblical faith and a church sharing in the powers of this world. Her thinking takes sides. Her only "bourgeois" characteristics are her exactness and precision, the reliability of her scholarship, and what might be described as an early-bourgeois modesty of expression. Over the years, this former school-teacher of mine, without whom I would never have ventured into theology, has become for me more and more the model of a teacher of hope.

Among those who have helped me I also count other Christians whom I came to know after the war; some of them had been in the resistance. They were rooted in the tradition of the Enlightenment. Because I could do nothing with a Christianity that demanded the acceptance of all kinds of miracles as supernatural events, I would never have moved beyond polite curiosity about Christianity without a dose of Enlightenment and demythologizing. I had to choose between an existential nihilism and an existential Christianity. If one could not go back to the ambivalences of the bourgeoisie, the only option for my generation within the traditions of the middle class was to become a nihilist. Nietzsche, Gottfried Benn, Heidegger, Albert Camus, and Sartre were our conversation partners.

But there *was* an alternative to this nihilism: There was the face of a man, tortured to death 2,000 years ago, who did not choose nihilism. Actually, it was Christ who got me into theology, Christ who forced me to ask the question, Can one really claim that all that matters is love? I knew that I had always felt drawn to human beings who served as models, people of passion and devotion, such as Maximilian Kolbe, who voluntarily went into the death-cell of Auschwitz in place of another inmate who had five children. It had already occurred to me that one loses one's soul through apathy.

I discovered Søren Kierkegaard when I was twenty. I was caught up in one of those deep crises of meaning and identity that haunt young people of our culture. It was 1949, and one of the philosophical responses of my generation to the recent events of Europe was existential nihilism. Kierkegaard was seen as the father of Sartre, Camus, and Heidegger, the fathers who articulated our stance. After reading the first twenty pages of Kierkegaard, I knew that he had something that the sons did not deliver: radical religion, transcendence over what is, a passion for the unconditional. But I did not know whether he was concealing this something, withholding or only indirectly expressing it.

Speaking about the foolish young women in the gospel who had the door slammed in their faces because they had no oil for their lamps, Kierkegaard said that they had become "unrecognizable in the spiritual sense because they had lost all infinite passion."

Kierkegaard seduced me into religion. I devoured him. Today I might say that I fell in love with Søren (Is there really a better way to learn anything?); back then I would have rejected such speech as inappropriate. But as I was reading, my fantasies and intense, months-long conversations with Søren took a totally unscholarly turn. If I had been Regine . . . Why did the engagement have to be broken? . . . What does sexuality mean when you have found your "category"? . . . Why does Søren, who is not really brutal or trivial, say these insulting things about women? I became engulfed in Kierkegaard.

At every reading I was fascinated by the outward arrogance and the inward humility of his style. Was arrogance not "only the allowed but, above all, God-pleasing and necessary self-defense against the insinuations of mediocrity?" And did it not require arrogance to make anxiety the central concern in the Copenhagen of 1844? The following sentence is from *The Concept of Dread*: "There is no anxiety in spiritlessness; it is too happy, too content, and too spiritless to know anxiety." Decades later I reread this sentence from an existential perspective by relating it to the religio-political situation in which I live, thinking about the NATO leaders, secretaries of defense, and politicians who govern my life. Indeed, there is no anxiety in spiritlessness.

Neither poet nor philosopher, Kierkegaard was a preacher in a secularized society, explaining and defending the Christian faith. This undertaking is no less absurd for a Christianity accommodated to the bourgeoisie than it is for a world geared up for business.

For Kierkegaard, dread belongs to the side of freedom, not to that of necessity; this insight was eminently important for me. I learned from him that we are wholly free only when "without dread we renounce dread," that is, when we believe. In the state of dread, we look for but then flee from guilt; in faith, we confess guilt. Dread-free, spiritless persons cannot believe, because nothing compels them to do so. They continue to cling to bombs and profit margins.

"To be in need of God is humanity's greatest perfection," is how theology puts it in one of its classic statements. What Kierkegaard taught me was that without experiencing and embracing dread, there is no way of becoming a human being. We may say that God somehow uses dread to lure us. Those who allow themselves to be caught by it, who are so marked by it that the most effective of detergents cannot remove it from the fabric of their being, are on God's fishing line.

Friedrich Gogarten was another of my teachers. Even though there is hardly one of his own basic ideas that I took up substantively and developed further, he was a marvelous instructor in the art of thinking. I encountered him not only in books but also in the lecture hall and seminar room. When I was nineteen, I read one of his books, *Die Verkündigung Jesu Christi* (*The Proclamation of Jesus Christ*). It was the first real book I was able to buy. Gogarten was one of the cofounders of "dialectical theology" and a leading participant in the secularization debate. The book was written in most idiosyncratic language. It advocated a basic theological principle that I readily absorbed: "Only in our own language" can we speak properly about God or Christ, "and not in one that has come down to us, just as in the case of everything else that belongs to our life and has reality in it." Some time later I heard him say that a "well-mannered" child is precisely one who has no "manner"; only the ill-mannered child has manner proper to itself—and it is an irreplaceable manner touched with audacity!

This theologian had a wonderful capacity for differentiating what is learned by rote and then parroted from what is experienced personally and then expressed, however haltingly. To Gogarten, the category of experience was very important. I recall how worked up he could get: One of the fashionable terms of the day was "eschatological"; apparently everything had to be "comprehended eschatologically." One day he declared, "Eschatological! I don't know what you want! I always picture a sausage that has no end." He demythologized terms and reduced them to what one could appropriate and then take the consequences.

One evening at university, in one of Göttingen's pubs, Gogarten confessed: "My God, how brazen we were!" At a conference, the topic for discussion was humankind's incapacity for the good. Returning home, a participant asked Gogarten as they waited on the platform in the train station: "But why should we not be capable of the good?" From the window of the train already in motion, Gogarten replied: "All it takes for me to answer that question is one look at you!"

Indeed, he could come across as highly arrogant. He told us of a particular conference when he had to share a hotel room with Paul Althaus, a theologian whom he subjected to sharp criticism. In the dark of night, while searching for the light switch, Althaus pushed the service bell instead. "You see, Herr Kollege," Gogarten said, "that is how you are: You want light, and instead you make noise."

That sort of critique, for which an apology was due, was no lapse. Often Gogarten turned this critical treatment on himself: "Did I really say something that stupid?" He enjoyed switching concepts and reformulating in a different terminology what he "meant to say." When a student, with the articulations of the previous term still ringing in his ears, merely regurgitated them without really grasping their meaning, Gogarten became quite unpleasant. In Göttingen, one was not raised to be a "well-mannered child."

Discourse was Gogarten's natural habitat, and he was a good, patient listener. Every Monday night, after his seminar, he invited a student to his home, where a meal and conversation were shared with him and his spouse. Later, it continued in his study, cut off from household activity by two thickly padded doors. Gogarten would stuff his pipe and grow silent. (Later he gave me one of his pipes, which I smoked for many a year.) He waited for the young student to raise his or her own questions. For decades he kept up this practice; the custom is virtually unimaginable in today's educational milieu. I relate this detail as evidence of what in philosophy is known as "personalism," the relationship between a You and an I, the mutuality of giving and receiving, the dialogical principle.

It is within this reality that I came to know what it means to have a teacher, an experience that appears to have become more and more rare. For what is a teacher? It is a human being whom I myself have chosen. Initially, you do not become a teacher as a result of your knowledge and wisdom, but because someone has chosen you to be his or her teacher. The teacher who has been assigned to me must have something to teach, not just specific knowledge but also knowledge that transcends her or him personally. However, a teacher also needs more than a discerning mind, understanding, and knowledge: she must stand for something, to testify to something. From her/him it should be discernible what one ought to love and what one ought to despise.

A connection with a live, practiced tradition can be made only when, beyond my subjective experience, I can place my trust in the teacher. That does not entail blindly acceding to the teacher's suggestions; rather, it means that one can overcome basic skepticism and suspicion—in old-fashioned language, I am obedient to the teacher, in the sense of heeding her word. I set out from the belief that the teacher does not intend to deceive me, whether through well-meant praise or indifferent, anger-free admonition. Instead, I rely on her to teach me by being and giving of who she really is.

Today, when I think of my teacher Friedrich Gogarten, what is most present to me is how often he met our doubts with words of assurance and that he taught us to behold reality with amazement.

Finally, he taught me an old German word I had not known: *Freidigkeit*. Luther had used it to translate the word *parrhesia* in the New Testament. It is often rendered as free openness, free-mindedness, venturesome confidence; Gogarten told us that it was a melding of "freedom" (*Freiheit*) and "brazenness" (*Frechheit*). Heaven help the student who interpreted this magnificent term with the clerical sentiment of "joyfulness." This would infuriate Gogarten, who utterly despised any kind of churchy drivel. But, at times, one may glimpse in theology the radiance of a fragment of this bold freedom, this *Freidigkeit*, which on the day of judgment is to be for us a sign of the love of God (1 John 4:17). Perhaps it was not just an unknown word that I learned from my old teacher.

... AND BECOMING A TEACHER

I studied classical philology, German, and philosophy in Cologne and Freiburg, and, after that, theology and literature in Göttingen. After graduating in 1954, I returned to my hometown where, for six years, I taught at the Genoveva School in Cologne-Mülheim. It was a decent, politically centrist school for girls, shaped by the spirit of the Roman Catholic Church. All my female and the few male colleagues naturally participated in the Corpus Christi procession.

On my second day there, I was on yard duty. An older teacher reprimanded me: "What are you doing out here? Hurry back to your classroom!" I looked very young, indistinguishable from my pupils; this often caused much laughter.

In those years, I learned quickly that in my school, where history ended in 1914, the story of German fascism was not taught in class. Some of the teachers had been touched by it, others had not and, never having studied it, did not know how to approach it. The easiest option was to keep quiet, and that is what they did.

One day, in trying to explain something to my fourteen-year-old pupils, I used the Nazis as an example. A week later, they said to me: "My father says that the Nazis were not really that bad; they built the Autobahn." I discovered that not only my class but the whole school population knew nothing of the Nazi era. Such was the reality of the 1950s.

A colleague (who later became a friend) joined me in making the most of the relative freedom we enjoyed in shaping the religious instruction curriculum. On our own, we came up with a lesson plan, and we taught grades five through thirteen about national socialism. When there were objections from the church authorities, we provided a pedagogical rationale for what we felt we had to do. To objections from the educational authorities, we responded with a theological rationale for our initiative. What an advantage to have to serve two masters!

In teaching about the Nazi years, I was once challenged by a very bright group of pupils. They served me with a long list of their parents' justifications for supporting Hitler: He got the unemployed off the streets, did away with inflation, reestablished law and order, and the like. By chance, in the Protestant religion class there were eighteen girls. In my desperation to get them to understand anything at all, I asked them to stand and number off in threes. "Now imagine," I said, "that all of you who said 'three' are going to be eliminated by gassing. There were eighteen million Jews in Europe before Hitler came." The moment was not forgotten.

During my tenure at Genoveva, I discovered Bertolt Brecht; he had not appeared in my studies of literary criticism, and his plays had been kept off many a West German stage. I loved him, particularly for his classic plays' female characters such as Mother Courage, Shen Te, and Grusche. What I found fascinating in Brecht was his forthright, down-to-earth affirmation of the dignity of the human being, even, for example, that of a useless "unworthy, old woman." I wanted others to be aware of this. My little book *Creative Disobedience* was to take shape some years later around this theme. In my teaching of religion, I often drew on Brecht—and it was a miracle, indeed, that I was allowed to continue at all.

A number of things became clear to me as I studied the conceptual foundations of fascism. For example, the first people to be sent to concentration camps were communists and socialists, but the church did nothing until its own people were affected. A friend and I discovered this only by going through the sources ourselves. All of a sudden, the so-called resistance of the churches was no longer as significant as we had been led to believe.

Although it was not obvious to me at the time, my move into theology had politically and historically much to do with my sense that, in responding to the events of 1933, liberal Protestantism had been helpless. This was the German culture of my parents, where one would read Goethe rather than the Bible. Despite liberal Protestants' inability to stop anything the Nazis did from 1939 onward, in 1945 a naïveté still prevailed among those who thought they could begin once again where they had left off twelve or more years earlier.

I began to ask why the German bourgeoisie had fallen apart and betrayed its liberal ideas and values. And how could parents and teachers assume that the bourgeois culture that had expired in Auschwitz was salvageable? What amount of rebuilding, re-educating, re-arming, reconstituting of previous conditions of ownership, and all the other "re-"s could ever save it? Were the Nazis not the very outcome of this German history?

Or, were they just a bad dream one could wake up from? How could there be hope for a reconnection without radical surgery?

For me, the German bourgeoisie's relationship to Christianity had been too aloof and indecisive, and still was. I was attracted by the high value Christianity put on every individual life: You can gain your life or you can lose it. With the apathetic or pre-political consciousness of the proverbial monkeys who do not wish to see or hear anything, let alone protest against anything, people can proceed to destroy human dignity.

My suspicions of postwar German public life were confirmed in how the Federal Republic of Germany developed. Chancellor Conrad Adenauer's policy of re-arming the Republic in the early fifties hit me hard; I could not fathom how it was possible for everything suddenly to become as it was before. So many of my university classmates who had fought in the war had, in endless, all-night sessions, told me of their experiences at the front, at Stalingrad. In my crowd were a number of older friends who used me, as we said then, as their "garbage can," so great was their need to unload the burden and dump their horrible experiences of war. "No more war, ever again!" was the prevailing sentiment in those years. And those who thought a bit further would add, "No more fascism, ever again!"

At about the same time, Adenauer offered West Germany an economic "miracle"—huge rivers of money, the Marshall Plan, industrial growth. All we had to do was renounce a piece of neutrality that so many were dreaming of and that nourished their hope for the reuniting of Germany. Instead, we got economic upturn, re-armament, and incorporation into the Western Alliance.

Now I was really hearing Pastor Martin Niemöller, a man who offered resistance against the Hitler regime, for the first time. I found myself attracted by a tiny group of people who were taking to the streets. I had a long conversation with my mother about the older peace movement. She was passionately opposed to war, and I have rarely seen her cry so terribly as in the summer of 1938 during the Czech crisis. For a well-ordered household like ours, she did something quite extraordinary: She woke up all five of us children in the middle of the night and announced that there would not be a war because British Prime Minister Neville Chamberlain had come to Munich and tamed the beast!

Our conversation now in the fifties focused on re-armament and what could be done to stop it. I said, "I'm going down to have a look at those people," to which my mother replied, "Go ahead, but you must know that it won't achieve one little bit." In light of two different considerations, I thought long and hard about that remark—especially later, when we blockaded the nuclear rocket sites at Mutlangen and elsewhere. I had no doubt that Mother was right. At the same time, I knew that I belonged "there," and belonged with those "crazies." I sensed even then that the label "success" is not one of ultimate value, that, as Martin Buber said, "Success is not one of God's names."

RUDOLF BULTMANN

Whenever I sent Rudolf Bultmann an article, he would always respond with a postcard. I have kept one that is signed: "with hearty, so to speak, grandfatherly greetings." I was very happy to have such accurate expressions of my relationship to this great theologian and I think of him with unfailing thankfulness. I did not have him as a teacher, but I regard myself as one of his granddaughters/students. Without Rudolf Bultmann, I would have found no access to theology and, what is infinitely more significant, no way to faith.

I was a child of the liberal Protestant bourgeoisie, with Immanual Kant and Wolfgang Goethe upstaging the Bible or Martin Luther, and I grew up in the climate of the Enlightenment. It was natural for me to have intellectual doubts about the substance of the church's teaching: Who cares about Virgin Birth, an empty tomb, miracles, and dogmas? But the man Jesus Christ in that tradition had a hold on me. The tradition of the church had disfigured this man from Nazareth: all those catechetical platitudes, those boring church services with their authoritarian claims, and finally, neoorthodoxy's assertion (to which we were exposed in religion classes) that God must be "wholly other" than our thoughts. Whatever substance there was to Christianity, I could not recognize it in such ecclesiastical packaging.

It was Rudolf Bultmann who spoke to where I was in my final high school years, up to 1949. From my teacher Marie Veit, I knew Bultmann to be a Christian hospitable to the Enlightenment. I need not leave my mind at the church door. Reading his work, I came to know this teacher as a man of incorruptible integrity, a thinker in the tradition of Gottfried Lessing, one who was intimidated by neither institutions like the church nor traditions like the Bible. Yet at the same time, as I was told, Bultmann was very religious, a professor of world renown who for many years used to collect the Sunday offering in the parish church of Marburg. How could these go together: thinking and believing, criticism and religiosity, reason and Christianity?

Bultmann answered such questions with his program of demythologizing. It signified that the Bible and subsequent Christian preaching derived from a world that was marked by mythic thinking. It had to be clearly acknowledged that its worldview is a thing of the past and that science had taken over from myth the role of explaining the world. One of Bultmann's well-known statements is that "one cannot make use of electricity and radio, rely on modern medicine in case of illness, and, at the same time, believe in the New Testament's world of spirits and miracles."

It was not Bultmann's intention to do away with or dissolve myth but to interpret it, so that the message of the Bible could also address the children of science. One cannot live with one foot in the age of science and the other in the world of myth. Such a contradiction empties reason of responsibility and makes faith an escape from reality. Therefore, the Bible needs to be "demythologized," that is, freed from the yoke of mythic thinking.

I, along with many others, experienced Bultmann's thinking as a liberation. In July 1942, Dietrich Bonhoeffer had written: "Bultmann let the cat out of the bag, not only for himself but for many more and I am glad about it. He dared to say what many (including me) suppress within themselves without having overcome it."

The cat is out of the mythological bag; the stories of Jesus' empty tomb and of his perhaps filmable resurrection are legends, media in which the first disciples expressed their faith, within the confines of their understanding of the world. If we take seriously what they want to tell, then we cannot simply repeat it after them; the mystery of faith and its power would die in such repetition, which includes within it the suppression of our doubts. This mystery of faith, in which people are freed from their past (wherein they seek to build their security) for the future of love, is what concerned Bultmann. As a teacher, again and again, he helped people to have the courage for piety and did so no less as a proponent of existence freed from the mythological.

Bultmann's thinking was the focus of discussion until the mid-'60s. He did not engage in the process that emerged then, which I call the politicization of Christian consciousness. My book *Political Theology*, in its German edition of 1971, bears the subtitle *Discussion with Rudolf Bultmann*. He made a substantial contribution to the clarification of the basic themes of my theology.

The term "political theology" is today almost commonplace in the language of church history. My book had grown out of what we had experienced in our "Political Evensong" in Cologne since 1968, the impact on us of the war in Vietnam, and the experiences of the student movement. It reflects the theoretical basis of our praxis at the end of the '60s.

In response to that book, Bultmann wrote me a four-page critical letter, from which I cite the following:

> I agree with you that specific changes in the social structures may reduce the constraints which today cause us to sin. But what does it mean to sin? According to my 'individualistic' understanding, there is no sin that is caused by the constraints of social structures. I mean by sin an offense of one person against another, for example, lying, abuse of trust, misleading, etc., but not as a collective failing of the command of the moment. You are right in what you intend; however, what you call sin I speak of as guilt. You do not distinguish between sin and guilt. I use your banana illustration as an example: There is a difference, surely, between killing or robbing a banana worker and getting my bananas through the United Fruit Company. If the banana worker is paid a pittance for his labor, he always has the option of striking or going to court.

I had to laugh and cry about that. Part of the greatness of liberal thinking is its hope; it represents a piece of the heritage we must hold on to. In this case, liberal hope is naïve and has not the slightest connection to reality—because this banana worker, this *campesino* and exploited slave, can neither strike nor go to court—but it does present us with a claim that is under no circumstances to be rejected.

Naturally, it is with skepticism and critique that I look upon these comments by Bultmann. In my judgment, the distinction between guilt and sin cannot be stated in a way that makes guilt a collective and sin an individual matter. I regard that to be an utterly false distinction, particularly in view of my experience of and reflection upon the fate of our people, the question of Germany's guilt and what it means to be German after Auschwitz. I can put into one word what it is that separates me from Bultmann: Auschwitz. My attempt to do theology is marked by the awareness that I live after Auschwitz. Bultmann, on the other hand, does his thinking within the confines of a bourgeois understanding of scholarship as objective and unrelated to the times.

One of the coincidences I have seen in all this is that it is precisely sin that we face here. In the reality of six million murdered Jews, we cannot distance ourselves from personal sin. My entire consciousness of sin, put simply, is based on the collective occurrences in my country, my city, my group. Of course, I am aware of individual sins of which I accuse myself, but I believe that they take up less room in my life. What I suffer from, and what I need and seek forgiveness for, are all the disastrous things that we, as a society, inflict today on the poorest of the poor and on our mother, the earth. For that I need something in addition to the indispensable analysis. I need a language other than that of explanation, definition, and critique in order to be at all able to show what is at issue. It is at this point that I believe I try to go a step beyond Bultmann, not backward into a biblicist naïveté, into a pre-critical world, but, after the passage through the Enlightenment, into a new language that we are now working on within the liberation theology we seek to develop.

Really great theology always practices narrative and prayer. I remember an address by Bultmann that caused us listeners to feel quite devotional. He argued and demonstrated that speaking from the lectern, in the academy, was not the same as preaching in church, that they were two different things. During the discussion afterward, someone said: "But what you just did was, for me, very much like praying." It had indeed been that. Bultmann did not want to believe it, but his theology was better than he thought; it had the quality of great theology in that it spoke in the various idioms of religion with a passion for the absolute. The language of religion is one of narrative, prayer, and argument.

Even though he put such a restriction on theology, I think that there are many places in his theology where Bultmann really prays, led to do so by the substance of theology itself and free of the fetters of cerebral argumentation. Whatever is living testimony of the life humans live today cannot be summed up in statistics and press releases. Prayer and narrative shun that form of communication; its inherent frigidity would kill them.

When I think about what Bultmann would say today concerning the validity of the mythic, I believe that it would be a yes and a no. No to myth—if it means a mere reversal to the irrational, to what is highly skillful and of great artistic significance, and at the same time a complete denial of whatever meaning the Enlightenment held for us. No to a myth whose power horrifies us but whose content we are no longer able to discern critically. Demythologizing is often a means of telling the truth about the bosses of this world. Yes to myth, if it is an eyes-wide-open engagement, a third step that leads out of naive belief, through the liberating, demythologizing critique, and into a reappropriation of the hope for all humanity that is promised in the myth.

STATIONS OF A
THEOLOGICAL BIOGRAPHY

In 1965, my first book, *Stellvertretung* (*Christ the Representative*), was published; it is a critical discussion of theological tradition and an attempt to articulate the meaning of Jesus for us today. Two basic assertions are made: The first and relatively traditional one is that Christ represents us before God like a lawyer represents an accused person before a judge. The second declares that Christ represents God among us, that is to say, the absent and invisible God, the God who perhaps has taken a trip, whom the majority of humans believe to be "dead." The subtitle expressed that perception: *An Essay in Theology after the 'Death of God.'* A reputable academic publisher in Göttingen, who had published my dissertation in the area of literary science, refused the manuscript on account of the subtitle. But I could not do without it.

The book was not intended to meet any career needs; it was meant primarily to help me reach clarity myself. I wrote it in the gloomy years of separation from my first partner in marriage, at first in the desperate hope that he would find his way back to me. Only a new relationship with a married man, with whom I wanted "to find a bit of shelter because it was so cold outside," gave me enough stability to begin writing again. Encouraged by the publication of some of my essays in *Merkur*, a "Journal for European Thought," I set out to find greater clarity. I struggled for every inch of theological territory: What can I really believe and say, what do I have to let go, and what do I want to let go?

I studied and discussed the "God is dead" or the "death of God" metaphor, especially in Jean Paul's marvelous work "Discourse of the Dead Christ from the Edifice of the World That There is No God," and the young Hegel. As a result, I got into trouble with the officialdom of the churches; many did not, or did not want to, understand what my concern was. Perhaps from their perspective it was not edifying.

I sought to clear away understandings of God that, like dead branches, still hung everywhere in Christianity and from which I wanted to be free. I sense very clearly that, as Teresa of Avila put it so well, God "has no other hands but ours" with which to accomplish things. It was simply impossible for me to think of a divine being, removed from the world, who would intervene with supernatural might. Such intervention always happens through us, that is, in the history of incarnation, to put it theologically. The life of Christ occurs in that Christ—not the historical Jesus but the Christ of faith—continues to incarnate himself, resisting the demons and suffering as a result. That is how I understand Pascal's famous statement: *"Jésus sera en agonie jusqu'à la fin du monde: il ne faut pas dormir pendant ce temps là."* ("Jesus will be in agony until the end of time; until then, we ought not to sleep.") God's history continues in and through us. To be precise, the abstracted, extraspatial and extratemporal God, who then somehow intervenes beyond our comprehension, is a kind of idol, a "God with us" on the belt buckles of the German armies of two world wars.

Like *Die Hinreise: Zur religiösen Erfahrung* (*Death by Bread Alone* is the U.S. title; *Inward Journey* the U.K. title) published in 1975, *Stellvertretung* contained numerous elements of mysticism. Mystics have always tried to conceive of God in ways different from the dominant churches of their time. In a more encompassing way, on the one hand, they always transcended the language of God. And in a more inward way, on the other, they put "God within me" into words. Mysticism surely was the language that helped me the most to find clarity here, in part because it does not shy away from feuding with a philosophical-metaphysical language of God. It is also much closer to the language of the Bible, which speaks of God not in dogmas but in narratives.

From the outset, my critics charged me with preaching that "God is dead" while incessantly using the word "God." That logical contradiction was not hard to detect. All I wanted to say was that we need God but not the "Mr. Fix-it" who manages everything "from above." To be in need of God is the human being's highest perfection; that is how I understand Kierkegaard. To me, letting go of that claim seemed tantamount to betraying the pain that keeps us alive. Within me, the insights of modernity and its worldview were at war with a sort of premodern yearning that in the course of my life has not become less significant but, rather, more essential. I *cannot* give up loving God "above all else, with my whole heart and all that is in me." It *is* necessary to speak of God, because there is a foundation of the world, a source of life or a truth that was there before us, that transcends us and allows us to look upon life as a gift on loan.

One can reflect on the difficulty of "believing in God atheistically" with the help of the concept of "power." The Swiss philosopher of culture, Jacob Burckhardt, once said that "all power is evil." This view is deeply rooted in Protestantism and I can understand why. I identified myself passionately with the powerless Christ. From beginning to end, my entry into theology was Christocentric; it did not proceed via God the Father but via the Son, the older brother. It would never have occurred to me to become a Christian if there had been no more than an almighty God. Power and powerlessness had to be understood differently than the tradition of interpretation. I saw "the powerlessness of God in the world" and tried to pursue further Dietrich Bonhoeffer's idea of our "participation" in that powerlessness.

Only gradually did a certain expansion take place within my theological biography, from this strictly Christocentric position toward a reflection on the ground of life, on God. Today I am more and more aware of how necessary this is in encounters with other religions, for example with Judaism and others who have been called not by Christ but, rather, by other voices of the God of many voices. This is a consistent move for me: trying to speak a new language in halting tones does not render us monotonous; it enables us to hear better. Indeed, for me Christ is God's clearest voice, but that meaning does not preclude other voices of the divine for other people, for example, Zen Buddhists. Not to understand this is to fall victim to religious imperialism.

In the European intellectual situation, three different phases of religion are identifiable. I call the first "the religion of the village"—we are born into it without being asked first. Most of us experience it in our childhood. The church is at the heart of the village; its authority, its rituals and sacraments, its norms and ethical values are beyond question. As people move away from the village, this inherited religion drops into oblivion or meets with rejection. The secular city, where the majority of us live, negates the customs and manners, traditions and songs of the village. For those who remain in the village, faith turns into superstition, hope into illusion. Religion is either forgotten or is the focus of intentional critique.

I myself was born into this second phase: separation from the inherited or compulsory, imposed religion. My parents were highly educated members of the German middle class, who manifested a certain "enlightened" tolerance toward the church. It was in keeping with my bourgeois and family background that I began my studies at university in philosophy and the classical languages. Provoked by a number of friends who were Christians by choice and, even more so, by radical Christian thinkers such as Pascal, Kierkegaard, and Simone Weil, I found myself, after the fifth semester, in an existential crisis that led me to take up theology. This change in the course of my studies marks the beginning of my transition from the second to the third phase.

To name this third, post-Enlightenment form of religion more accurately is one of the tasks I have set for myself as a theological writer. I have no nostalgia for the village, nor do I feel at home in the chill of the big cities. This religiosity is different, because it is individually and freely chosen. I am not a Protestant because my parents were but because I chose to follow this tradition. That means that I also have the right to make choices within the tradition, to be selective. I do not have to swallow every word of the Bible, including those hostile to women. Religion in this third form is voluntary; it has a clear grasp of its minority status, free of dreams of omnipotence. It seeks to serve rather than rule.

If I were to look within my sphere of experience to find where such a religion is a lived reality, I would point to the Protestant church in the former German Democratic Republic. The externally imposed renunciation of power did not lead to the death of the church and religion but rather to self-clarification, objectivity, and modesty. The term "church within socialism," signaling a departure from the pro-capitalistic church many had longed for, has today become historically outdated. In my view, it was a step in the right direction. It would certainly clear things up if the churches in Germany—but not only in Germany—were to understand themselves as "churches *within* capitalism."

The term "liberation theology" describes best the kind of radical Christianity within which people from the broad *oekumene* have found one another and now, from their diverse origins and in their different dialects, work together for the same goals.

In the course of time, my understanding of theology has taken on a certain anti-academic tone. This is a result not least of the numerous attempts of people at the base to make the biblical tradition their own in their work in the peace and ecology movements. It was my belief that theology should reflect people's faith where it is alive and practiced and that it should help people to clarify faith. The conversation partners of theologians, their interlocutors, are the groups in the congregations—the women's and peace movements, those working on issues relating to ecology and refugees—seeking to live as Christians.

My theological fathers, like Karl Barth and Rudolf Bultmann, still spent much time and energy working in local congregations, attending ministers' conferences, or answering letters of irate pastors. They were there for the church, whereas the partners of today's theological masters are other academics, for example, in the fields of natural science. Their theology is done in the form of consultation at the summit level; groups like the women doing South African solidarity work have no place there. I continue to be drawn to the church as a community of solidarity, faith, and struggle. In many ways, I regard theology's sidling up to the sciences as a counterproductive step. In the face of what really goes on in the world, what are the brightest minds of West German theology doing in long debates about how scientific theology can or should be? They are making use of the sharpest, finest knives they can find to split hairs as thinly as they can.

This phenomenon becomes apparent to me in answering the questions: What issues do I have in mind when I occupy myself with the Bible? What is important for me and why do I do this? Luise Schottroff once told me how, at the end of the '70s, during a meeting of one of the more illustrious scholarly societies, she proposed the study of poverty in the New Testament. There was only embarrassed silence, because no younger scholars in New Testament studies wanted to jeopardize their academic future with that kind of topic, particularly in Germany. Even though this subject is present on every page of the New Testament, one knows only too well that making poverty the subject of scholarly study may lead to unpleasant consequences.

Although it needs aspects of science, theology is much more akin to praxis, poetry, and art than to science. For centuries the better theologians were more artist than scientist. I think of Michelangelo's portrayal of Adam in his depiction of creation in the Sistine Chapel and how, being touched by God, Adam awakens to life. Eve is already placed near God, in God's embrace. Theologically more interesting authors like Gottfried Lessing, Johann Georg Hamann, Blaise Pascal, and Franz Kafka tend to make use of language in a different way. That is the kind of theology I have in mind when I imagine a theological kingdom of God, although I assume that in such a kingdom there is no need of theology.

POLITICAL EVENSONG

The "Political Evensong" was the experiment of a group of people who wanted to put into practice the statement that faith and politics are inseparable. It was our first expression of a search for *oekumene* from below. The question of one's origin—Catholic, Protestant, or whatever—appeared as unimportant to us as that of a person's dialect. This is, of course, not a meaningless question, since it does provide a certain degree of coloring, but it is far from being essential.

One Saturday evening, when we had celebrated communion together, a close woman friend asked Fulbert, my future marriage partner, who at the time was still a member of the Benedictine community in Maria Laach: "Do you think that I have to attend mass tomorrow?" When Fulbert told me about this later, I was horrified that something that had long ceased to be a concern for me was still an issue for others, and particularly for someone who was a dear friend. We later answered this question as a group: The reality of God's Spirit leads people out of false questions.

When we began our work with this group in 1968, I was teaching German Studies at the University of Cologne, and I was the mother of three children. Originating in friendships between a number of Protestant and Catholic Christians, some of whom were clergy and others who had studied or were interested in theology, our group met in social gatherings at night. Our membership changed, and guests from near and far came and went. We had theological discussions about new forms of the creed, marriage, and new understandings of the sacraments.

We soon realized that our preoccupation with theological questions would not lead to commitment without engagement in what the "Republican Club," as we called ourselves, named as "burning actuality." In the winter of 1967–68, the war in Vietnam was such an actuality. A number of actions resulted from the engagement of members of the group: the discussion on the Vietnam War on the doorsteps of St. Alban's Church; the distribution of leaflets that were reprinted subsequently in other cities; the Good Friday worship service in the new marketplace of Cologne, where for the first time we tested the genre of political prayer. At that point we were not sure whether we should call our action a teach-in, go-in, or a procession.

By then the ecumenical group had grown from about a dozen to nearly thirty members—thirty Christians who understood more and more plainly that theological reflection without political consequences was tantamount to blasphemy. I put it this way: Every theological statement has to be at the same time a political one. We applied for the opportunity to present our liturgy during the Convocation of Catholics in the city of Essen in 1968. We were scheduled for a time after 11 P.M., which gave rise to our prayer services being called "evensongs." Our pattern was to provide political information integrated with biblical texts, a brief address, calls for action, and finally, discussion with the gathered congregation. The basic elements of all subsequent Evensongs were information, meditation, and action.

This community of people was randomly composed. The tasks to which people could put their diverse talents in their specific contexts were wide-ranging: selecting the topics to be addressed, gathering relevant information, composing the prayers, negotiating with the ecclesiastical authority for the use of their spaces, advertising this new form of worship service with the help of the press, and so forth. In Cologne we experienced how the weak ones in the group became strong when they let themselves be drawn into the organizing process. It appeared useful that every group preparing for an Evensong drew on the expertise of someone well acquainted with the selected topic. But one did not have to be an expert to put information together, plan an action, and write prayers. The subjects of our worship services were to be as precise, circumscribed, and concrete as possible. The more circumscribed the topic, the stronger the possibility to provide exact information; the more concrete the topic, the more fruitful the discussion and action.

What emerged was a series of worship services with a wide range of topics: the invasion of Czechoslovakia, Santo Domingo, and Vietnam, discrimination, death, authoritarian structures in the church, discrimination against women, real estate speculation, participation in decision-making, the German Democratic Republic, the administration of prison sentences, development aid, faith and politics, and so forth.

On October 2, 1968, the newspaper *Kölner Stadt-Anzeiger* published an account of the Political Evensong:

As early as 8 P.M. last night, the church of St. Anthony's was filled to overflowing. At 8:30 the parish clergy announced that there were a lot of people outside trying to get in. "Let's move closer together, it is a good sign for an ecumenical worship service." More than 1,000 people showed up for the Political Evensong in the Protestant church that can hardly seat 300. There were Catholic chaplains, Protestant ministers, students, politically engaged people like the Vietnam Circle or the Friends of Biafra. After the words of welcome by the parish clergy, the members of the ecumenical working group took over the conduct of the Political Evensong. Father Fulbert from the Benedictine Monastery in Maria Laach invited those present together to design in discussion the shape the political prayer was to take. As if in theological seminar, many in the audience wrote down the final texts. There were no disruptions, even though there had been anonymous telephone threats beforehand.

Right from the outset, the Political Evensong was exposed to the cross-fire of all sorts of opinions. Even the confession of faith I recited on October 1, 1968 in Cologne aroused critique and countercritique. The moderator of one church called it heresy that should not be heard in a church, while others regarded it as a respectable personal credal affirmation.

CREDO

> I believe in God
> who created the world not ready-made
> like a thing that must forever stay what it is,
> who does not govern according to eternal laws
> that have perpetual validity,
> nor according to natural orders
> of poor and rich,
> experts and ignoramuses,
> people who dominate and people subjected.
> I believe in God
> who desires the counter-arguments of the living
> and the alteration of every condition
> through our work
> through our politics.

I believe in Jesus Christ
who was right when he
"as an individual who can't do anything"
just like us
worked to alter every condition
and came to grief in so doing.
Looking to him I discern
how our intelligence is crippled,
our imagination suffocates,
and our exertion is in vain,
because we do not live as he did.

Every day I am afraid
that he died for nothing
because he is buried in our churches,
because we have betrayed his revolution
in our obedience to and fear
of the authorities.
I believe in Jesus Christ
who is resurrected into our life
so that we shall be free
from prejudice and presumptuousness,
from fear and hate
and push his revolution onward
and toward his reign.

I believe in the Spirit
who came into the world with Jesus,
in the communion of all peoples
and our responsibility for
what will become of our earth:
a valley of tears, hunger, and violence
or the city of God.
I believe in the just peace
that can be created,
in the possibility of meaningful life
for all humankind,
in the future of this world of God.
Amen.

Naturally, there was a price to pay for the inherent proximity to socialism, the linking of Christianity and politics that many people found scandalous. Once our group had begun this work, almost all its members experienced unexpected problems in their own contexts. Neighbors stopped greeting them, conversations ceased, friendships dissolved, business connections were broken off. Some were verbally assaulted and pushed off sidewalks when they were distributing leaflets; many noticed that the announcements of upcoming Political Evensongs posted in schools or universities were defaced or ripped down. When answering the telephone, my children were told: "Tell your mother that she is a pig, a communist pig." It was news to me then that a fascist sentiment of rage and hate still existed in our society.

What was experienced by the student movement was now also happening to adult working citizens. There were repressive actions; such actions issued from the remarkable consensus of the two major churches, Protestant and Catholic: access to space denied, false reporting, verbal harassment, pressure on the media, relocation of young clergy or refusal to employ them. Cases of these repercussions on clergy multiplied in both churches: chaplains at vocational schools who informed trainees about their rights were relocated by the church, pressured by the companies who had placed apprentices in these schools.

The harshness with which church authorities moved against leftist theologians varied from one regional church in Germany to another, according to the Protestant diversity in that country. Still, it was enough for authorities to consider someone who had collaborated with the Political Evensong "untenable" and, accordingly, "ineligible for employment."

VIETNAM, MON AMOUR

It was in the context of the Vietnam War that an important phase of my evolution from liberalism to radical-democratic socialism took place. Like the Spanish Civil War in the '30s, the Vietnam War represented a massive encroachment on the Left, profoundly affecting the lives of many European intellectuals. I was fortunate to have a friend, Erich Wulff, who worked in Vietnam as a medical doctor. His yearly vacations in Europe meant that from the early '60s, I heard more and more about what was really going on in Vietnam.

Erich Wulff later wrote the important book *Vietnamesische Lehrjahre* (*Vietnamese Apprenticeship*) using the pseudonym Georg Alsheimer. In it he described his own conversion from liberal to socialist. From the many stories and details of this capable observer, I could really form a picture. Showing why one could find no middle ground nor remain neutral in Vietnam, he became more and more politicized. We came to understand many problems in developing countries in light of this context. "Third World," "neocolonialism," "dependency theory," and other words that are now common currency were coined at that time. All this we learned from the example of Vietnam, a country whose leader, Ho Chi Minh, had composed a constitution based on that of the United States. When the French left Vietnam, people honestly believed that—with the consent of the Americans—there would be free elections. It was not to be so; instead, the Americans came marching in.

I discovered, as if for the first time, the country under whose rule we were living. The negative dimension related to imperialism; the positive connection in the fact that the best information available to us for resisting the Vietnam War came from the Quakers of North America. They were fearless, truth-loving Christians who sent us excellent analytical materials.

When we distributed our information, we were constantly harassed and told, "That's just communist propaganda." It was so helpful when we could show that "No, this was written by Quakers from Wisconsin." I learned a lot from this, including the prejudices of my own class, family, and background. A clash between my mother and me was predictable. She said: "How can you be so anti-American? After all, they liberated us from Hitler." She was quite right, of course, but I had never understood that to oppose Lyndon Johnson or Richard Nixon or others—in historical perspective, surely murderers—was explicitly anti-American.

Our time of struggle coincided with the student movement. I found the movement wonderful; all of a sudden, we were so many. I had become used to the fact that we were so few and far between that you had to look long and hard to spot a like-minded person. Everywhere, you were little, ugly, and insignificant; you could get hardly anything published. Difficulty was omnipresent.

This feeling had worn me out, particularly in the peace movement, where I spent so much of my energy. But suddenly, many people thought the same and understood everything. I would never have thought it possible that in Germany so many people would see things the same way and draw the same conclusions from what they saw. For this change, we owe thanks to the people of Vietnam, who resisted an overwhelmingly powerful foe in an exemplary way. I have felt a deep love for Vietnam ever since; it has become part of my life. What those people did for humankind and also for me is enormous.

It all began with a conversation I had with Erich Wulff in which he told me that the Americans themselves did not torture people. They stood next to the torturers from other Asian nations, tape-recorders in hand, recording the extorted confessions of the Vietcong and subsequently incorporating the data into the theory of guerrilla warfare and counter-insurgency. Throughout that all-night conversation, my defenses were up: This cannot be true, you are mistaken, you lie, this is propaganda, Americans don't do such things. But I had to accept the truth of what he reported, and much more that I would have scarcely believed possible. I realized that as a German, belonging to a people with experience in the administration of torture, I should know where such things happen and to what purpose.

In the next years, Vietnam became very close to me; I studied the liberation movements, the theory of imperialism, and the analyses of what was happening in developing countries. The Vietnam War also helped me to see my own history from a new perspective: Auschwitz did not end with the war; it continued—that was the lesson to be learned. It has never left me. This realization became the decisive moment for identifying myself even more with socialism. Our Political Evensong also grew from this experience and so, subsequently, did the European section of Christians for Socialism.

By late fall of 1972, peace in Vietnam, which to many of us had seemed close at hand, once again slipped away. The secret talks in Paris between the United States and North Vietnam failed. Then I read in the newspapers and heard on the radio that the United States had resumed the aerial war against North Vietnam. In a major attack, it had bombed the cities of Hanoi and Haiphong.

Just before that, I had been in Vietnam with a delegation of a nongovernmental organization (NGO) for assistance to Vietnam and had informed myself about the effects of the war. I put my impressions on paper. It was a report of my experiences, but it did not say everything about the Vietnam War. While the Western media informed us daily about South Vietnam, as a rule we learned very little about the North.

> It was raining; we had driven to Haiphong to see the city. In the hospital built by the Czechoslovakian-Vietnamese Friendship organization, we saw baby Fung Mink Tuk and the bomb-splinter in his head. Even before he was born, his life was threatened; his whole family was buried alive in an air-raid shelter. He was born after many of the civilian population had been evacuated from the city, and on August 15, 1972, barely three weeks old, he was wounded as his mother held him in her arms. His grandmother was killed, his mother and older sister wounded. His brain injury had festered; the abscess and splinter had to be removed surgically. And, given the child's age, that was extremely difficult even under normal conditions, without high alert, aerial attacks, and blockades.
>
> We could see everything the doctors accomplished in this clinic—there were no windows or doors left, and the floor was covered with bomb and shell splinters. A doctor told us: "We were just performing an operation when the nurses' residence was hit. The air pressure threw us against the wall, metal fragments flying around us. A doctor's aide was wounded. Now our work has doubled."
>
> Most of the children in this hospital had been wounded by what was described to us as a *bombe perforante,* a "penetrating bomb," which before it explodes first drills itself some thirty inches deep into a building or underground bunker. It cannot do

any damage to concrete or stone buildings; it was designed especially to destroy people. It disintegrates into very small, difficult-to-remove fragments, which enter the lung or liver. Between April 16 and October 1, 1972, 75,000 such bombs were dropped on Haiphong alone.

We stood in a hospital room with eight beds and listened to the soft voice of the chief physician telling stories of patients and the fate imposed on a small, agrarian people by the state-of-the-art inventions of the greatest superpower.

A member of the provisional revolutionary government, who had been held from 1957 to 1962 in a variety of camps and prisons of the Saigon government, told us about "tiger cages," cells twelve feet long and four and a half feet wide, in which from eighteen to thirty-two persons were held. When the door was closed, it was pitch-dark inside. Many did not know where the floor was—they were lying on top of each other. Except for a pair of shorts, they were permitted no clothes. A small box served as a toilet. Only when five people had passed out were the others allowed to knock and call for a guard.

I asked him: "What if you were to meet one of your torturers now? What would you do? Would you treat him the same way?" He raised his hands, deflecting the question. "We differ from those people. Often, they did not act as they would have wished. Often, they were coerced to do so by the aggressor. But if they go with us now and fight for the people, we are ready to give them our hand. If they go on with such crimes, we shall punish them; if they change, we won't."

I had often been asked about my personal reasons for engagement on behalf of Vietnam. That land had become a laboratory where state-of-the-art weapons were tested on human beings. Again and again a picture I had seen came before my eyes. It was of a Vietnamese woman trying to escape the napalm by wading through a river. On her back she carried a child about five years of age. I thought, even if the child survives, the fear and the damage can never be erased. And sometimes when I looked at my children, who were then fifteen, fourteen, eleven, and nearly two years old, I remembered that child. I realized that "motherliness" is indivisible; one cannot be a mother to one or two or three children and that's it. One cannot like a few children and forget about the children in a school who were incinerated in an American bombing raid because it was believed that the Vietcong were hiding there. One cannot write them off as the regrettable victims of military necessity. One cannot care for a few children while supporting a policy that incinerates so many children, that lets them starve or rot in camps.

Another reason I became involved with Vietnam was both personal and Christian. I thought that I had known what it meant when I had said, "I am a Christian." In those words I expressed a relationship to a human being who lived 2,000 years ago and who spoke the truth. I tried to take that man seriously, because I believed that his story has implications to this very day.

I could find no difference worth mentioning between a crown of thorns and these tear-gas derivatives that under unfavorable wind conditions cause you not only to cry and vomit but also to suffocate. I could find no difference worth mentioning between the newly tested shells and poisons and the ancient technique of killing by crucifixion.

The Vietnam War did two things for my generation: Like nothing else before, it unmasked capitalism. And, at the same time, the Vietnamese people—representative of other peoples—gave us the gift of a new vision of life, of the future.

The American antiwar movement played a very significant part for me. It was shaped extensively by Christians, not only by Quakers and the traditional peace churches but also by the "established" or "mainline" churches. This broad movement stimulated the civil rights and environmental movements. This has given me a deep fascination with the United States, so much so that when I moved there, I felt intimations of homecoming. In Western Europe, the pacifist movement, the civil rights movement, and Christianity were often very detached from each other. There I had the feeling that when I was among socialists, including those in solidarity work with Vietnam, I almost had to apologize for being a Christian. But in the United States, it was taken for granted; a radical Christian tradition lives there. Political radicalism blossomed forth from Christianity and traveled with it.

THE LEFT—WHAT ELSE?

When asked about my political orientation, I give the ready and laconic answer: the Left—what else?

For me, becoming more radical has theological and political dimensions, if those words are not too grand. To me they mean growth in devoutness and in revolutionary consciousness. If black slave-women and their by-no-means freed grandchildren could sing, "Lord, I want to be like Jesus," we, too, perhaps need to be less afraid of such grand words.

A key experience on my way to being radicalized was the realization that these two dimensions of radicalism cannot be separated from each other. Existentially, radicalization does not permit us to put one ahead of the other. We shall no more transform first the heart and then the world than the other way around. "Seek first the reign of God *and* its justice" (Matt. 6:33). This is the theological-political radicalization to which I dedicated decades of my work.

I come out of a milieu that was not familiar with socialism. From the educated bourgeoisie I had to follow several detours to arrive at my embrace of the leftist vision of justice. In the convulsion of my generation, I had chosen Christianity; it never occurred to me to connect that with the working class or any other "wretched of the earth." What I did understand was that the spiritual foundation of my parents, this bourgeois liberalism, was not enough. It had led us into the disaster of the Hitler years, or at least it had something to do with it. I felt how mistaken it was to dismiss Hitler as if some sort of tempest had blown in from the outside, from this Austrian housepainter, swept over us, and had moved on. The roots were much deeper, and I dug them up one after the other.

Later, I often became impatient when Christian believers asked me, "Are you a Marxist?" The best reply that came to mind was this counterquestion: "Do you brush your teeth? I mean, now that the toothbrush has been invented?" How could you read Amos and Isaiah and not Karl Marx and Friedrich Engels? That would amount to being ungrateful to a God who sends prophets among us with the message that to know Yahweh means to do justice. Do we not have to make use of every analytical tool that helps us both to comprehend the sources of injustice? Should we not recognize at the same time that victims of injustice are the possible forces for the change that breaks the yoke of oppression of both victim and perpetrator? Could we afford to ignore Marx in a time when it should be clear to every attentive observer of the misery of developing countries that capitalism is neither able nor willing to end hunger?

What guided me in this work was recognition that our economic system works for the world's richest people but excludes the vast majority of the human family. Shouldn't we who stand in the tradition of religion, with its anthropological concepts of the dignity of the human being, at least look around for a historical alternative? For me the need for a thorough analysis arose from the biblical faith in a God of justice. It appeared to me that an education in theology that does not incorporate an economic theory betrays its own purposes.

Like a subversive stream, the cooperation of Christians, socialists, and other humanists dogs the postwar history of the ever increasingly militarized Federal Republic of Germany. In my life, both the re-arming of Germany and the resistance of the "first peace movement" were very important moments. I joined communists and socialists for the first time in this "war against nuclear death."

We learned to understand our own tradition in a new way. We finally opened ourselves to one of the greatest intellectual challenges to faith and stopped regarding Marxism as an enemy's invasion into our peaceful, harmonious territory. Thomas Mann once called anticommunism "the greatest folly of the century." After nearly one hundred years of hatred, fear, self-deception, defamation, and lies, Christians, too, came out of their shelter and entered the dialogue with socialism.

Did we bourgeois or petit-bourgeois intellectuals have any right at all to lay claim to the traditions of the working class? Could we simply shed our skin and relinquish our privileges?

In this question I learned much from the French left. Jean-Paul Sartre coined the phrase of the necessary "betrayal of one's own class." In conversation with my sister and brothers and my mother, I often felt like a traitor. One of Louis Althusser's basic ideas helped me in the Evensong discussions about social location. This French Marxist made an interesting distinction between class-situation and class-position. The *situation de classe* is a matter of birth, of fate. It is not my fault that I had had educated, liberal parents. This situation must be distinguished from the decisions one makes about life, the relations of solidarity into which one enters, and the obligations that become important and determine one's position. In this sense of a *position de classe*, I would say that I am a Christian socialist. The theoretical discussions began at the end of the '60s and with the student movement; I am thinking of the "Marienbad Dialogues." They emerged chiefly from Austria's Roman Catholicism; women were more or less absent from those discussions. I never went there, but the topics that were discussed and eventually published were important to me; for example, the question of whether a Christian can be a socialist at all, that is, whether there is a socialism that lets go of atheism as one of its tenets, or whether every form of socialism presupposes atheism. It was a lengthy discussion; today this question has become obsolete in view of the theology of liberation developed outside of Europe. Liberation movements have developed an understanding of religion that has nothing to do with "the opiate of the people." What will remain of Karl Marx is not his critique of bourgeois religion but his challenges to the idol of the free market.

At the beginning of the '70s, a number of people in Salvador Allende Gossens's Chile came together to form the Christians for Socialism. I remember a major meeting, in 1972, of the Evensong circles from the Netherlands, Switzerland, and various cities in West Germany. We discussed how our work was to continue and what we might call ourselves. There was a seemingly endless debate about "Religious Socialists," "Christian Socialists," or "Red Morning Star." On the last day of the meeting, two Chilean priests joined us; they belonged to the group Christians for Socialism. They told us that two members of their group had been murdered in the stadium of Santiago. Our debate came to a sudden stop; it was utterly clear to us all that we would adopt that name for our own: Christians for Socialism.

We should not forget that the beginnings of Christian-Marxist dialogue, as well as of such groups as Christians for Socialism and others, did not occur in conference centers. They began in fascist prisons and concentration camps where Christians and Marxists met, sharing suffering and hope, cigarettes and news. The dialogue among intellectuals, at least in Europe, where it started in the '60s, was a latecomer.

In developing countries, the dialogue began under fundamentally different conditions. Behind the meeting of Christians and Marxists lay the historical experience that neither religion nor socialism can be rooted out by sheer force. In the countries of Eastern Europe, religion not only continued to exist but even increased in its significance; socialism could not be killed by the concentration camps of the fascists or the machinations of the CIA. This is how I put it in the late '70s; it is an insight that I want to maintain even today after the collapse of socialism.

In my experience, the Christian-Marxist dialogue was a time of growing together and mutual learning. In numerous gatherings, I not only became familiar with socioeconomic analyses of various kinds but also found that my theology underwent a transformation. Together with a growing number of reflective Christians, including those from the conservative camp, I finally began to recognize our own contribution—as rich consumers—to the different forms of oppression.

Especially in developing countries, Christians increasingly joined the liberation movements or, at least, participated in groups that fought against the brutal violation of human rights. In many places, a new Christian-socialist identity came into being.

What did we learn from all this? I express the answer theologically: We came to know, in a new way, the meaning of incarnation—both in theory and in practice. The encounter with Marxism deepened my Christian understanding of the historical and social dimension of human existence.

Often the God of Christians is no more than a noncorporeal, heavenly being above and beyond history's victories and defeats and is experienced exclusively by individuals in connection with their individual fortunes. This God lives in the realm of ideas and has neither a bodily nor a social dimension. It is a deity who certainly wants to have nothing to do with whatever happens to the body, to material society, and to social structures. In confronting philosophical materialism, I have learned to take material existence more seriously in its twofold sense of body and society. In this manner, hunger and unemployment, and the military-industrial complex and its impact on day-to-day life moved from the periphery to the forefront of my theological work.

I began to understand God's becoming human no longer as a unique, completed event, but as an ongoing process in history. In this process God is rendered invisible (as in Auschwitz), or is made manifest in the experiences of liberation. Marxists have helped Christians to understand better the deep this-sidedness of the Christian faith of which Dietrich Bonhoeffer spoke.

This dialogue between Christians and Marxists came to an abrupt end in 1968, when Soviet troops marched into Prague and suppressed what Alexander Dubček called "socialism with a human face." It was a frightening defeat for all of us who, like him, dreamed of a human socialism. The dialogues immediately halted; some of the Eastern participants were jailed, faced harsh reprisals and threats, and were thereby silenced. The historical attempt to reconcile Marxism and democracy one to another was crushed by one of the imperialistic superpowers. A similar event would happen four years later in Chile as a result of the efforts of the other superpower.

Then came a strong headwind. Within the Catholic church, the most progressive and open positions taken by the Second Vatican Council were revised. They were watered down and, yes, abrogated. The Catholic reform movement in the Netherlands, which in the beginning of the '70s had experienced such a remarkable spring, was suppressed and smashed by Rome. Priests were relocated if they resisted, and Catholic publishing houses were prevented from publishing radical writings. The progressive Catholic newspaper *Publik* was shut down. Pope Paul VI steered a much more rigid course than had John XXIII. The time of hope seemed over. Everything grew numb.

Yet, in the meantime, other forms of cooperation between Christians and Marxists began to grow. This came less from intellectuals, professors, and journalists than from people in resistance groups engaged in the political and social problems of the West and countries dominated by the West. Among such problems were the accelerating deterioration of living conditions, inflation, unemployment, and ecological crisis, as well as the war in Vietnam and the overt or covert military and financial support it had. The most important resistance offered was perhaps that against the economic exploitation of developing countries. In the '70s, socialists and Christians more and more frequently found each other to be allies in their various forms of struggle.

People throughout developing countries experienced in this dialogue a coming together that was much more than theoretical. In those countries, especially in Latin America, the intelligentsia is strongly anti-clerical, while the "ordinary" people are Christian. This difference was often overcome in their practical work. The fact that a large proportion of the "minor clergy," such as the local priest and the nuns at the health clinic, are on the side of the people is known to us from European history. Before the French Revolution, the upper clergy stood with the rulers, while the lower clergy was associated with the people.

Therefore, the Christian-socialist dialogue was not simply "broken off"; it was relocated. It went into the torture chambers of Latin America and lived on in different places and under a different historical reality.

Must a Christian be a socialist? In the mid-'70s, a German weekly newspaper discussed that question for weeks; two decades earlier, it would have been unthinkable to raise such a question.

The people who learned in the school of alliance for struggle drew in equal measure from the Christian and Marxist traditions. It became more and more troublesome and senseless for them always to separate what motivated them and to distinguish their goals as "Christian" or "socialist." In many groups, this process went beyond what the individually inherited linguistic and symbolic worlds might suggest. When asked by a radio reporter from Arizona whether I supported the struggle of the sanctuary movement for political or religious reasons, I countered by asking whether he had ever read the Bible. If yes, how could he ask such a question? Was Jesus, in his opinion, a refugee for political or religious reasons when his parents took him to Egypt in order to save him from the death squads of King Herod? And was Jesus crucified for religious or political reasons? The more I read the Bible, the less I understood such questions.

Christians have often been accused of being useful stooges of the Bolsheviks, but the reality of liberation theology contradicts this fear. Christians were in no way instrumentalized in the service of an ideology that believed itself to be all-knowing; the reverse is much more true: Christians made use of the relevant instruments of liberation provided by Marxist theory. We used the tools of analysis: critique of exploitation, class struggle, false consciousness, and the like. We found in these concepts splendid aids in the comprehension of reality. We did not use them to create a new ideology that associated itself with "scientific atheism," the leadership role of the all-knowing and all-powerful party, or the suspension of the human rights of the class enemy.

The theology of liberation in which I was engaged took from Marxism whatever helped in bringing about changes; it re-instrumentalized theology instead of ideologizing it. The biblical concept of "the poor" makes this abundantly plain. Liberation theologians took it up rather than talk of "the subproletariat," "the marginalized," or "the revolutionary class." The more encompassing concept of the poor embraces the dignity of these human beings and affirms the fact that they are God's most beloved children.

In the ecological theology that was to emerge later, we spoke in similar ways of creation instead of nature, in order to express the intrinsic value of the created that cannot be instrumentalized or assigned a price. A chicken is there to lay eggs; that is its instrumental value. But it also has the right to scurry about and to cluck; it has an intrinsic right to life, as do all creatures. This example shows, perhaps, how far away we were from an orthodox Marxism that had rigidified into an ideology. The distance was evident not only in the question of the indivisibility of human rights but also in a number of philosophical presuppositions about the role of nature as the arsenal and object of human exploitation. As Karl Marx himself put it: *"Moi, je ne suis pas Marxiste!"* ("Me, I'm no Marxist!")

TO LOVE BACH IN A
WORLD OF TORTURE

"To Love Bach in a World of Torture" is the title I gave to an address I delivered in conjunction with the Nuremberg Organ Festival. The invitation to speak had put me between a rock and a hard place; a predicament typical of my life, it seems. I began work on my speech by trying to acquaint myself somewhat with literature on the music and aesthetics of Johann Sebastian Bach. Then I received a call from friends who were working with refugees from Chile. They were asking me to fly to Santiago as part of a European delegation. They wanted me to gather firsthand information on the hunger strike staged by relatives of "disappeared" persons. What was I to do? Should I stay at my desk, meditating on suffering, the arts, and theology? Should I fly to Santiago to be with people who had been tortured themselves, or who waited in the hope that a torture victim might still be returned to them? My decision to join the delegation to Chile had consequences for the Nuremberg address. Speaking as someone whose preparation was more existential than scholarly, I addressed the question of deciding between religion, politics, and culture. This dilemma is one that very often forces itself upon us today. I try to conduct my life so that I may respond in sympathy and with concern for others; this is where music helps me, almost more than anything else. But I do not want to decide between them, to make a choice. For how could I love Bach, while accommodating myself to torture, even if that accommodation merely meant managing temporarily to forget about torture?

The SS bosses in Auschwitz gassed people and then went home and listened to Beethoven with no problem. For them there was no contradiction in what they experienced as two discrete phenomena. This example may seem extreme. Yet is this dichotomizing, this separation of one thing from (or after) another, not one of the most deeply rooted characteristics of our culture? I despair more and more of this modern culture of division, subdivision, and irreconciliation.

If this separating of spheres of life a characteristic of bourgeois culture, the new, post-bourgeois interest might well be to liberate both the arts and religion from their subjectivistic privatization and to turn them once again into media of communication and collective memory. Theology, the arts, and music are engaged in the archaic endeavor not to abandon language about what affects us most deeply but instead to foster communication among ourselves. Both theology and music make suffering less mute, isolated, animalistic, or petrified. They both move us to let tears flow.

And so my Nuremberg address became a continuation of Theodor W. Adorno's well-known essay of 1951, "A Defense of Bach against His Admirers." Adorno seeks to free Bach's works from the clutches of the 1950s' cultural conservatism. Adorno writes about people who are either incapable of, or no longer accustomed to, faith and self-determination; he says they invoke Bach because they are looking for authority or want to feel secure. This critique of the reception of a "neo-religious Bach," is not to be regarded as a fundamental critique of religion. What Adorno is taking to task is a religiosity without substance, one of piety for authority and lust for security. This is the religiosity in which the very stuff of religion is celebrated with a ceremoniousness that disconnects people from the rest of their lives.

Bach's piety is part of the warm current that flows from the Protestantism of Martin Luther, in which the church as institution does not occupy the center. It is in his understanding of suffering that Bach's piety is Lutheran. The arias and recitatives of St. Matthew's Passion are of the highest musical expressiveness; they give the terse biblical text a unique depth of feeling: shame, sorrow, pain, and joy come into their own.

Here is where great difficulties arise for an existential appropriation today. As a central element, musically speaking, the arias are utterly necessary. But what effect do they have on the Passion and its drama, given that both vocally and instrumentally, they are often laden with the sweetness of infatuation? Does this not rob Jesus' pain, suffering, and death precisely of the very reality without which nothing whatsoever can be appropriated of what the story of his death under the horrible weight of the Roman Empire's torture truly signifies? In addition to defending Bach against his admirers, do we not need to defend Christ against those who render him harmless, especially when they use Bach to do so?

Again and again when I listen to St. Matthew's Passion, I catch myself looking for something, as if there were another hidden dimension. It is as if this music challenged me to bring to it something it does not supply itself but demands of me. It is as if the St. Matthew's Passion of Bach were unfinished because we cannot keep up with it; it is as if it were unfit for our appropriation because we cannot digest its fruit until we ourselves have passed through the stations of our own road.

Listening to the oratorio, I become part of the story, joining in the indignant cries of the disciples, "Let him go! Stop! Do not bind him!" I hear, and my inner eye is opened. What does this music do with me? It touches me, it moves me, and it teaches me; it leads me into reality: "*O Mensch, bewein dein Sünde gross.*" ("Bemoan, humans, your great sin.") This music makes me feel and see what I did not feel and had preferred not to see at all.

NEW YORK, N.Y.

It was with a mixture of curiosity and criticism that I accepted the invitation to teach systematic theology at Union Theological Seminary in New York City in 1975. My one previous visit to the United States had been brief, and so, like many a European intellectual, I arrived with prejudgments. In many respects, I was supercritical, even snobbish. I learned to my amazement that in this city there were nearly thirty annual performances of St. Matthew's Passion and close to one hundred of Handel's *Messiah*. I had no idea that I was coming into a cultural capital.

It was surprising to me how my prejudicial expectations were disappointed. There is a kind of European cultural imperialism, a snobbery perhaps, that is also very much at home in the German universities, particularly in the long-established disciplines of the humanities and theology. Resting on their traditions, some European intellectuals assume that different methods and questions cannot really amount to anything. It is no different in everyday life. I spent my first week in New York with two young women who lived in my house. Bristling with full-blown anti-Americanism, they declared that there was just no decent food to be had in this country; everything is loaded with chemicals, sugar, artificial additives. No decent meat! In the ensuing exchanges, I suddenly found myself defending the Americans and advising my young friends to first look more closely in order to see what possibilities offered themselves here.

The three of us thoroughly altered our prejudgments, acknowledging that in spite of the abundance of all kinds of junk, much in the United States is truly great. Perhaps my first positive impression was the size of the country, in terms of the scope of possibilities and the opportunity to test them, to "give something new a chance," as one of the many American sayings puts it. Upon my arrival, my colleagues and acquaintances commended my fresh, new insight. I was flabbergasted; the word "fresh" seemed utterly inappropriate to me. But it was being used in a deeper sense: Here you have not yet been put to the test, so let's wait and see how far you can get with what you have to offer.

I arrived in an America that had just ended the Vietnam War and had finished with President Nixon. Unconsciously I looked at every man of the middle generation with the question, Were you in Vietnam? What did you do there? Vietnam had been such an elemental aspect of my own political and human biography. What was your position on the war in Vietnam? I could not put this question behind me, and even when it was unspoken, I judged many people in terms of it.

While in Europe, I had underestimated how widespread the middle ground was. On the one hand, one knew of President Nixon, General Westmoreland, and other figures who seemed almost fascist. On the other hand, one was aware of people who were opposed to these men. But the obvious fact of the existence of millions of people in between, refusing to see this as their problem, escaped me for some time.

In conversations with my new American friends who had worked in the resistance, I came to understand that there could be no neutrality in this matter. Many Germans had also believed this: that in the moment they had always conducted themselves correctly. This sort of prepolitical innocence was taken away from the Americans by that war in far-off Asia.

Also surprising to me were the reactions to my work as a teacher in a university setting. On several occasions I would deliver an address in the United States that I had first delivered in Germany; in the academic world, this is common practice. I found the reactions of American and German audiences remarkably different. In the academic milieu of Germany, listeners more often than not focused on perceived weaknesses in my arguments and sought to break them open. In contrast to this rather destructive orientation, the academic ethos in the U.S. was more pragmatic. For me the response patterns were therapeutic. If you come along with a key, they ask what it is good for, what doors does it unlock? They want to see if and how it works. Once my U.S. listeners were launched in this vein, their critique could be very sharp. The usually polite tone did not always mean much. I welcomed this pragmatic counterpoint and found it productive. The atmosphere was pleasant and less competitive than in Europe.

There was also a difference in the students. I learned right away that the relationship between learners and teachers was hardly comparable to that in Germany. Since in the United States there exists no traditional authority, or very little of it, there is no need to kill the authority. There is no need to dispose of the father, when right away, as a matter of course, one addresses him by his first name. The student-teacher relationship,

which includes mutual critique, is much more immediate. Students con-
tinually telephoned the office: May I come to see you, speak with you for
half an hour? In the first months, when my students became aware of the
relative limits of my acquaintance with English-language literature, they
came and helped me out, bringing a steady supply of books and whole
reading lists.

For the most part, the Union students were older. They brought
diverse experiences: the Vietnam War and resistance to it, the Civil Rights
Movement, the business world. They came from a variety of jobs: taxi-
driving, hairdressing, teaching, car assembly. A number of women were
entering a third phase of life, following college and marriage. Returning
to school was a liberating move, an attempt to rebuild a fulfilling life.
Many such women had experienced the phase of marriage and family
negatively in terms of their personal development and spiritual and emotional growth.

I found it wholesome to experience being at square one and unable to
presuppose anything. The students were altogether so different. For
example, one could not simply say, "As Kant has already maintained . . . "
At Union, one could assume nothing in terms of a general level of learning or canon of teachings. The student from Korea would ask in response:
"Yes, and do you also know what Sung maintained?" I did not even know
who Sung was. The Japanese, Australians, and the African Americans confronted me with their utterly different traditions. It would have been altogether grotesque to have them encounter Kant and Hegel without much
ado.

It struck me that the alienation that university study draws people
into was less severe, less coercive than in Germany. Compared with my
theology students in Germany, students at Union were able to raise their
personal questions, worries, and hopes more.

The manner in which the students approached problems, and the
subjectivity of their questioning, appeared very productive to me. To use
a somewhat romantic expression: They went in search of ancestors, of a
tradition with which to identify and from which to draw strength. There
was a strong feeling, particularly among African Americans, that history
had been written by the conquerors and that the conquered still had to
learn to write their own history.

One student wanted to write an essay about Christian anarchism. "I
don't know what you mean," I said to him, "but it would not be at all bad
if there were such a thing." He described the anarchism that began to

develop in Bohemia in the fifteenth and sixteenth centuries. He pursued it from there to groups in the U.S. and to communitarian movements and then related it to his commune in the Lower East Side, where he lived with ten other people. All of them were nonviolent anarchists who tried to counteract the landlords who tended to let their properties go to ruin. Such was the motivation of students who raised subjective questions— very different from those whose questions are purged of every trace of subjectivity and are only objectivist.

The seminary where I taught has the reputation of being a place of rebelliousness. Some evangelicals referred to it as liberal, or what was seen to be the utmost form of liberal, namely, communist. To read the Bible critically was paramount to being communist. That is an exaggeration of course, but people were indeed radicalized at Union Theological Seminary. Conversion is held to be a central theme of American piety; it is an occasion when the grace of God grasps a person usually associated with a specific moment in the person's life. From this theological tradition, however, arose questions relating to how one's political awareness came about. Many people have experienced a similar event, a theological-political conversion.

I was often asked what had radicalized me, what had taken me on this particular road. Why not earlier? And who are you now? Such questions made me tell my story, which I found to be a very productive, open-minded point of departure.

Then came the surprising discovery that fairly turned my understanding of U.S. culture upside down: the prevailing opposition against the culture of this country. What a few years ago had been called "counterculture" was by no means dead, even though it no longer appeared in the mass media to the same degree. I came to know many people who, despairing in the existing values of their culture, not only thought critically but also lived out their critique. They repudiated what were held up as essential factors: career, money, compulsive consumerism, and perhaps sexual achievement or commodified sex. Those people tried to live an alternative life, renouncing particular consumer goods and particular forms of human interaction. This counterculture also exercised a traditional role in the churches, namely, to create free spaces for the outsiders of society. Just as beggars or criminals in the Middle Ages found shelter in the churches, so dropouts or people who had broken with traditional lifestyles often found a piece of home there. Congregations opened their churches and houses and granted sanctuary to refugees and asylum seekers.

I experienced the religious openness to political and social questions that exists in the U.S. as a creative element in my theological work as well. I was able to learn a lot from the diverse religions, texts, and traditions there. One of the first books I came across was called *Liberation Prayer Book*. Published in Berkeley and originating from the '60s movements there, it set out to give new form to existing texts. It contained litanies with long lists of "saints"; people like Albert Einstein, Teresa of Avila, Mohandas Gandhi, and others who were implored to stand with us. If one wanted to criticize the book, one might say that it was a huge supermarket of religion, where everything was available for one to buy. But that speaks only at face value, because the book is an attempt to live life with the consciousness of a contemporary human being, for whom Einstein is sometimes more important than Moses. It tried to express such a consciousness in a language that keeps open the possibility for transcendence.

In this context, I experienced a considerable amount of "syncretism," as it is pejoratively called in Germany and other places. It appeared liberating to me. This reality of new religiosity was fascinating, as was the intersection of Zen Buddhism, Christianity, and mysticism, and how it is experienced in exemplary figures; here, Christ is one among the older brothers.

In New York, I also experienced, for the first time in my life, a quite sensuous liturgy. In Germany, we had conducted the Political Evensongs, but they had been distinctively marked by analysis, reflection, and documentation, a labor of consciousness-raising. The feeling that life is worth living, that we are to glory in it and praise it, did not really grasp me until I came to the U.S. "Celebrate" is a word that plays a significant part in that country, including in the domain of religion. People even spoke of "celebrating our sexuality," something nearly impossible, even linguistically, in Germany.

We lived in New York for two years as a family with two children. After that, we moved to Hamburg, and in the spring of every year, I returned to the seminary in New York for three and a half months. In those long times I learned how utterly alone one can be in that huge city. New York and loneliness: At times it meant a hectic search for entertainment, culture; I would read the theater pages of the *New York Times*, looking for something, and then make telephone calls, only to end up staying at home with classical or modern music. In honor of my classical radio station, I wrote the following poem:

Whenever I hear music on the radio
classical one-o-four point three
I feel afraid of the pauses
my tongue gets dry
I hear the silence
I hear the emptiness
in a time
that is not mine
nor that of Johann Sebastian or Johannes
or of the sad little Franz of Vienna

A short time
wherein I forget to breathe
because I am afraid
that soon the Wall Street report will assault me
and wretched counsel
what I am to buy
where I am to eat
how to invest my money
will beat upon me

I feel as if I had to protect my friends
Johannes from Hamburg
and Ludwig from Bonn
and Philipp Emanuel
(my God, he was already melancholic enough)
I do believe you
that you love them
but I still want to protect them
from your terror
of buying, eating, and investing money

That short quiet time
I believe that my colleagues
from classical one-o-four point three
could make use of it
because forgive me we need time
to love one another
especially Gustav and Robert
all of whom knew something

of the silence of the last note
of that peculiar time
that belongs to nobody
and is absolutely free
if you understand that word

Trying to find something, telephoning friends and then several theaters, and hearing "sold out" or getting no answer at all were part of the forsakenness of New York. One constantly had the feeling of having missed something, of things not seen, heard, or experienced. Surely one can be more alone in that city than on the remotest island. Then I would go again to Harlem and Canaan Baptist Church, a black congregation. Some of the spirituals were kept alive by the beat and the electronic organ. The slow, heavy singing and the sorrow it bears elicited all great emotions: confidence, hope, strength—*"there is power, there is power, there is power in the blood of the lamb."* I cried, and asked myself why. For one reason, I could imagine no white German congregation that expressed so much of being at home, so much community and responsibility; it is as if we are spiritually disabled. But there were surely other reasons to cry.

And then all the farewells and the change of continents. In my New York diary there is the following entry for December 20, 1986, one of my "last days" in New York:

My last day here. I read more steadily improving student papers and dish out more and more "with distinctions."

The memorial celebration for Heinrich Böll was held this evening at the German House of New York University. All five speakers—Kurt Vonnegut, Joan Davies, two older German Jews, and I—are trained in the forms of literature, speak briefly and reflectively, subjectively, avoiding any idle talk. One of the old professors of German Studies confesses that he actually had not wished to read anything from Germany ever again. In 1947 he had been forced to read this young, unknown writer from the Rhineland. It is as if Hein [Böll] had reconciled him—perhaps that is too big a word—with our dreadful country. The whole evening represents a peculiar mixture of interest in Germany after the Holocaust, and in that good human being from the Severin district of Cologne.

He radiates an authority the religious background of which most people hardly notice. In this secular company and the subsequent, long reception, I feel quite isolated. "Ah, you do theology? How unusual!" At the same time, I feel stronger than they, more knowing, superior, as if these people had no ground on which to stand. For some strange reason, this rather arrogant feeling stays with me.

Around 11 P.M. I ramble through the Village. The subway station is closed and I have to walk six blocks, a somewhat uncanny necessity. There are many beggars on the street, mostly black, mostly old. "God bless you," says one of them after I give him something. Perhaps the poor are the only people who understand what it is we talk of in our big words. Most of the time I can hardly bear to hear "God."

Walking through the night is like a farewell. Home again, I listen again to some music, Schumann and Rachmaninov, and read the last essay; it deals with the mistica revolucionaria *in Latin America. Even things I know fairly well become clearer here. At least some have understood better than I, the teacher, what I had really intended by offering a course on "mysticism and resistance." They describe the dark night of St. John of the Cross and the night of the people and quote a woman from Nicaragua who, after the revolution, declared: "Something in me was excavated."*

Good-bye, Babylon on the Hudson. Good-bye, my spiritual orphans, you students. Good-bye, compañeras. *Someone tonight said that Böll had been labeled a provincial by literary critics, but in reality he was international. I sense in me a little bit of envy for a sort of provincial home that I do not have. But then who really wishes such a thing as to be fully "at home" in this world?*

HALF THE SKY

I became a feminist through the agency of my American women friends. After reading my books in English translation, they campaigned that I be called to Union Theological Seminary. When I could not free myself promptly to get to New York by their invitation, I was calmly told that they would come to me. And so, in the spring of 1975, there arrived at our place in Cologne-Braunsfeld a German-speaking professor and an older female student, who spoke in a Southern accent that I simply could not understand. Both were members of the selection committee; the seminary had paid for the student's trip.

I owe it to Beverly Harrison that I received the call to Union. She taught ethics at U.T.S. It is no exaggeration to speak of her as a mother of feminist theology. Tirelessly she supports, counsels, and stimulates women in theology, organizes meetings and conferences. She critiques sexism in all shapes or forms and goes after every personal and institutional manifestation of the exclusion of women. Bev was the first of my women friends in New York.

SEVEN PARADOXES FOR BEVERLY

You are younger than I
but when someone came on to me recently
in a particularly mean way
I said you just wait I'll get my big sister

You have no children
But your apartment declares merrily
children wanted come one come all

Once I saw you crying
with rage about an injustice
but you were stronger than the strong

You think about abortion
but I have never seen a teacher
who drives away so little of life

Sometimes you are so buried in work
that I cannot see your face
but I have learned something
it is like the moon it returns again

Once I saw you crying
with happiness there is no paradox for that
once I saw you crying
and was happy

Sometimes I am sad
because I sense a thin wall between us
but it has doors

Beverly and the many younger women at Union who worked with me
as tutors asked me again and again what my theology has to do with my
being a woman. For a long time, I interpreted my theology more politically than in any other way. I understood it as a question of my national
identity in this century. Doing theology after Auschwitz had to mean
something different from doing it before. In the United States, I began
many of my speeches by saying: "I come from Germany. . . ."

I was not aware that this historical sensibility and the refusal to paper
it over with tools of scholarship might have something to do with my
being a woman. I simply could not suppress certain questions and topics.
For some reason, I had not learned the basic lessons of the German university: If, unfortunately, you happen to be female, then you have to
adjust, to submit; the topics you choose must be rigorously scholarly; you
must align yourself with prevailing methodology.

Another question my new American women friends asked was: Why
is it that you, one of the best-known German theologians, do not have a
professorship in your own country? I would reply by citing a newspaper
headline in the *Frankfurter Rundschau*: "Leftist and a woman—that's going
too far." The story concerned a conflict in 1974, between me and the faculty of theology at Mainz, who tried to get rid of me and eliminate my
unpaid teaching position.

Through discussion groups, and various other events in New York, I
became aware of new elements of feminist culture. I was cheered by book-

store signs such as "Feminist spoken here," seminar aphorisms such as "When God made man, she was only practicing," or, a particular favorite, "A woman without a man is like a fish without a bicycle." These manifestations gave me a better understanding of a number of things in my own biography.

Coming from a liberal home where intellectual labor was always respected and housework was equally shared by all five children, I had little consciousness of the oppression of women. I was the daughter of a very alert and spiritually independent mother. She raved about the wild '20s and sang us songs from *Threepenny Opera*. She subscribed to the journal *Die Frau (The Woman)* until its publication was forbidden. Scoffing at the Nazis' "Mother's Cross," she somehow managed to avoid having that "honor" bestowed on her. Of all her children, I resembled her the most and was her favorite child. Only by hearsay did I know anything of what Betty Friedan described in the '50s as "the feminine mystique."

Why did I not become a professor in Germany? The reasons certainly had to do with sexism, politics, and church theology—three factors that are well-suited to each other. I cannot say that I feel particularly bitter about this. For me, the combination of independent writing and a professorship at a very liberal theological school in the United States was actually ideal.

My apparent noncareer may also be the function of a certain woman-specific "late start," and a less than ordered way of life. As a woman and a mother, I have experienced various dimensions of this late starting. Usually, men's careers develop smoothly: One attends school, goes on to university, graduates, and proceeds up the ladder. But this "normal" process is different for most women: They get married in between, have children, possibly go through a divorce, live in other relationships. Their lives proceed with more complications. I often felt like a bird on the ground: A woman walks about on this man's land as clumsily as a duck and is just as awkward.

Perhaps the university had its difficulties with me because I took diverging paths, in search of a way of writing that was different from that of established scholarship. I did not want to overload my books with footnotes; I wanted to document my thought process, not my knowledge. The dominant pattern is to line up as many authorities as possible behind oneself instead of risking saying something new. I was often told, "Once again you are making quite a daring hypothesis!" I could feel the nervousness.

I think that self-protectiveness inhibits self-expression and creativity. Sooner or later, I have to decide what I really want. Is it to be safe at any price, protected by every footnote and acknowledging every authority? What is it that I seek to do by writing? Are there not other ways to access reality and make it visible? Even if less assured, there may be ways to provide greater chances to change people.

These internal difficulties surfaced in the course of my habilitation in the faculty of philosophy of the University of Cologne. My written work had been accepted to the point of one remaining formality—an oral presentation to and examination by the entire faculty. As an experienced public speaker, I entered the room without undue anxiety. I was about to say, "Ladies and Gentlemen," when I noticed that the audience of nearly sixty people did not include the two or three female members of faculty. After a moment's hesitation, I said, "Gentlemen." I sensed that everybody could read my mind.

What had not happened in Cologne since 1945 happened that day: I failed the "examination." A short time before, the right-wing organization, "Bund für die Freiheit der Wissenschaft" (Association for the Freedom of Science), had established a chapter in Cologne and become highly organized. Through my work in the Political Evensong, I had become well-known. I saw no reason to restrict myself while preparing for the habilitation. But this was held against me: My activity was said to trespass against the academic doctrine that the pursuit of science demands asceticism. Later it was reported to me that one of the professors present had remarked on my gall in having had a baby only two months earlier. This may have been unsubstantiated gossip, but it taught me something about misogyny, birth envy, and the fear of the "stronger" sex. Three months later, I repeated the examination and, thanks especially to Professor Walter Hinck, succeeded in passing it.

Of course, I was not spared the dilemma of "children versus work." All my conscious life, I resisted guilt trips about combining my own work with the tasks of domestic life. Young women should realize this is a false either-or. I was very clear about wanting to have children, living with a partner, and exercising my vocation. One of my best friends during the Cologne years, for example, was a mother of eight who was also a professor and politically engaged in the Political Evensong.

I had to have a job to support my family. My first marriage partner was a painter. He painted wonderful abstracts but did not know how to "sell" himself. This did not bother us too much, partly because I found much joy in being a teacher. But ever since, I cannot imagine myself being without work.

After my divorce, I lived without a partner for a few years. I had three children by then and made do in a thousand little ways. Now and then I had an *au pair* and was able to work at my desk at home. Both my mother and my former partner's mother lived in Cologne. I tried out every option available to me at the time except for one that I came to comprehend only later.

A few years ago, I visited a young woman who, after separating from her husband, lived with her children together with two other young women. Recalling my own experience of marital separation and the very hard times of single parenthood, I concluded that young women today are much further ahead, that something of the women's movement has taken hold. For them, life without a partner need not be a life alone; friendships with women are highly valued. These young women resist being isolated, and they seem free of the social complexes I had at their age. It took me years simply to tell the pediatrician calmly that my husband and I were living apart and that I was responsible for the children, and to ask him, please, to put my name on the invoice, that I would then pay. It was hard for me to develop the degree of self-awareness required to say these words in a society where one feels guilty for the failure of a marriage.

I worked for a time as an assistant in the philosophy department of the Institute of Technology in Aachen. I had to be there two days a week, Monday and Tuesday. Without fail, one of my children would get sick on Sunday night, a textbook case, with fever and pain.

Desperately, I searched for solutions. During these months, the conflicts with my mother were a heavy burden. She said that I could not have everything, that I had to be there for the children. Yet in this I was quite radical; it was a matter of course for me that to renounce work and other interests was a mistake. Was being a mother something that one had to pursue with a kind of self-destruction? I found this idea unacceptable and still do. I tried to make time for the children, with fairy tales, songs, and jokes. It did not seem to me the greatest of misfortunes that they ate fish sticks and not gourmet cooking.

Of course, it was a balancing act; it took a lot of skill, organizational talent, effort, and imagination. There were difficulties and defeats. One lunchtime conversation focused on what they wanted to be in later life. In a cheeky tone, my then-most-difficult daughter declared: "I'm not going to be anything. I will be a mother!" I had to swallow hard.

My husband and I now divide the work of the home among ourselves. For a time we would cook together or take turns; in the last few years, he has slowly taken over this task. I enjoy working in the garden, albeit without extensive know-how. Work is meaningful for me when my abilities are maximally involved, including physical abilities. I do not wish to be active only with my mind.

I have four children. Were I a young woman today, I would still decide to have children. However strongly I critique patriarchy, my feminism is not separatist in relation to men. I understand the importance of separatism for some women who need to come together and restructure their lives in women-only groups. But after recovery from the damages inflicted by patriarchy, the tasks of humanity remain to be addressed in common with men.

Perhaps my image of a happy life is less individualistic than that of many young women. I think that we need a certain kind of dependence in order to live, but not total emotional and economic dependence, the inability to organize our lives ourselves. There is a dependence that grows inside freedom: I could live by myself, but I want to live with you, enter into mutuality. The concept of dependence is often devalued in the women's movement; in whatever case, it is seen as deadly, as destructive of human beings. I find this wrong; I believe that mutual dependence is part of being human. Concretely, it means that I am sexually, spiritually, and emotionally dependent on others. I need conversation, challenge, critique, affection, understanding, and help in managing everyday life. I want to share my experiences with someone; I wish to give and to receive comfort.

While of little or no help for one's career or professional life, oppression is not without "advantages." Being nurtured to be quiet and listen is sensitizing, and therefore humanizing. Female socialization can engender pride and not weeping. Living in wholeness and having the desire to be united with or to give oneself to someone are assets in the process of becoming human. Holding back, not allowing feelings to surface, and seeking to spare oneself are liabilities of male socialization. After all, why is male culture so bleak and dreadful? Surely it's because men have resisted and destroyed so many female components within themselves.

One November evening in New York in 1985, I experienced in an exemplary way how feminism may acquire diverse accents. Two male students who had wanted to come and listen were not permitted to attend an event in the women's center of our seminary. As I learned only that evening, the center was restricted to women. I was very annoyed but did not cancel the event. Instead, I spoke for some time about separation.

What is to become of feminism, I wondered, when women act like racists? Subsequently, I wrote an open letter to the women's center and titled it "This is not my feminism":

> When I agreed to talk in the Women's Center about "Living and Dying in Nicaragua," I did not know that this lovely place is a "women only" space. I felt embarrassed and ashamed when men who wanted to listen were turned away. I knew that my sisters in Nicaragua would not and could not agree to a "politics of separation."
>
> What sort of feminism is behind this rule? I am aware of my own and other women's need for a special place for women at certain points in our lives. I understand a certain temporary separateness we need. It has to do with defining who we are, with the search for our identities. But when separation becomes separatism, the rule rather than the exception, something is lost in the integrity of our struggle. Feminism then becomes a biological category, another breed of racism. It then excludes men indiscriminately just because they have penises, as racists exclude people of a color other than their own. Feminism to me is a human enterprise and a necessity. Women as well as men cannot become human beings without struggling for liberation. And as women are not born into feminism and values, but have to learn them, so men are not excluded by nature. Indeed, God needs all her children to be freed from fear and hate so that we may finally grow into a space free from domination.

What has become more important to me than pure emancipation is that I do not want to divide myself. Emancipation is defined primarily by what it seeks to leave behind. The new women's movement, however, goes beyond that and expects more from life than to free itself from dependence on men. It seeks a different kind of life, a different culture. It seeks to establish different human relationships. It wants to have a differently structured world. It is well known that we do not want half the cake; we want to bake completely new cakes.

If one tries to picture the human being holistically, one doesn't develop only the half that is given to partnership, so that only there does enrichment, refinement, formation, and sensitizing take place. This would mean that the other half, which is given to individual self-realization in and through work, would remain behind at the level of the dominant culture and its barbarism.

To love and to work is an attempt, on the basis of a theology of creation, to engage in a new reflection on how human beings are needed. Even the best of partnered relations does not take the place of reasonable work. It is in this sense that my thinking is feminist. In retrospect, I would say that the books and projects that I composed before I engaged in feminism were already, albeit unconsciously, feminist, "*avant la lettre*," as the French put it.

In the '60s, I wrote a sustained critique of the God who keeps everything in order and who governs as a superpower that also allows Auschwitz to happen. The book's title is *Christ the Representative: An Essay of Theology after the Death of God*. It was a theology after the death of God because I was neither willing nor able to receive another piece of bread from this God. It was not clear to me at that time that it was actually a feminist-thinking theology and that my being a woman had something to do with my theological point of departure and critique.

Perhaps my road took a different course than that of many younger women for whom feminism comes first, and only then their politicization. I see them as closely interwoven: Having once tasted even a few drops of freedom anywhere in a world of slavery, stupidification, and being kept down, one necessarily thirsts for more freedom. And this crying out more loudly for more freedom is such a vital drive that the different forms it takes in movements of protest and resistance have today become integrated.

The women's movement, the peace movement, the ecology movement, movements of solidarity with developing countries, and others have, since the '80s, been called the new social movements. When I consider what these movements are all about, I notice that all of this ferment grows more and more together in my life and in my observations. They lead me toward a different, less materialistic culture in which people are not judged solely by what they earn. There is a culture where other values matter, such as being related to other human beings or being fulfilled in one's work.

A countercultural movement does not strive for what others already have. Rather, it seeks something new, precisely what the others do not have and what within their frame of reference is unthinkable. Such a movement rises up against the dominant and prescribed values of this culture, that is, against its materialism, its lust for war, its exploitation of the whole world, its destruction of nature, and its poverty of feeling. The wind blows into the face of such a movement, yes, but every headwind has its own upward draft.

THE PAIN OF BIRTH

My grandmother gave birth to her first child for three days and nights; in the end, forceps were used to deliver the infant. Five years later—her husband being what was then called "considerate"—she had her second child. That birth, too, was long and painful. When she learned from the midwife that it was a girl, she sighed deeply and said: "You poor little thing, now you will also have to go through all this." My grandmother told me this herself.

My mother bore five children, the first two in her small home (but already with the assistance of ether), the last three in a hospital. Her relationship to the pain of childbirth was sober, rational, and conscious: What is natural simply cannot be wrong, demonic, or evil. In our family, the word "natural" was highly regarded; whatever appeared unnatural, artificial, or affected had negative connotations. It was taken for granted that human work was to be much respected and that such respect extended to my mother's hard work of giving birth. The pain of childbirth is *labor*, hard physical birth.

How clearly I remember when my first child arrived; at first I hardly noticed the long-awaited labor pains. Then it seemed as if those pains, the whole toiling drudgery, were taking up residence within me.

The little apparatus with the laughing gas did not help me; it seemed to be much more a theraputic plaything of the medical industry. What did help was the preparatory breathing I had learned—deep, conscious, and self-controlled. This was an exercise of breathing with, rather than against, a labor pain. When the pains intensified, I lost out, of course, but at least it gave me some task and orientation. Above all, in between pains, it took away my fear of the oncoming pain. I have borne four children, but my memory of the pain has faded. The inexpressible horror that my grandmother experienced before and in childbirth is something I have been told about but never felt myself.

My daughter's experience in bringing two children into this world was very different. The protracted labor of the first birth used up all her

74 DOROTHEE SOELLE

strength and energy. "It is as if I had climbed up and down Mount Everest twice," as she put it. Afterward she was hungry and totally exhausted. The second child came in two and a half hours; there was much less exertion, but the pain was worse, more violent.

I recount this family history in order to call up in my mind the pain of birthing. I want to remember: I belong to a long history of women. It was important to me that I was present when my daughter's labor pains began. To "stand by" someone is a good term that expresses participation and compassion. At the same time, it also signals that there is a boundary inasmuch as the pain cannot be transferred from one to the other. Another woman or another man can be no more than a "bystander" to the one giving birth. It is a humanizing moment in the long history of nontransferable pain that when my daughter gave birth, her marriage partner was present.

I wish to note—but only at the level of theoretical reflection—that men's experience and memory of pain is insufficient for understanding pain, or just writing the history of the human perception of pain. My concern is how the experience has differed historically, as in my own case, which spans the history of the women in one family over nearly a century. How was the basic experience of giving life to a child understood during that period? How was that experience managed in the different phases of medical history? How did conditions change?

I was horrified to learn that for a time in middle-class circles in the U.S., cesarean sections were performed as a sort of fashionable procedure, when not medically indicated. Why on earth eliminate the anxiety of pain technologically, by surgical intervention, which often brings more pain in its aftermath? An operation takes the place of a birth—as if there were no difference. Why does the one giving birth become a hospital patient, she and her exertion replaced by a male operator who frees her from her work?

It is not easy to convey my outrage about this and other technological practices of eliminating anxieties. My horror is incomprehensible to those who automatically look at pain with a technician's eye. They see pain as an avoidable hazard, a senseless drudgery that belongs to the past.

Why am I frightened by the notion of a cesarean section for all women who still intend to give birth? And why am I disgusted and nauseated by the prospect of a science-fiction utopia of genetically engineered fertilization, that lets you pick up your baby at a laboratory, ready to go? Was it not bad enough that my grandmother had to suffer as she did? What meaning is there in the archaic suffering that the God of Genesis imposed on women at the expulsion from paradise? "I will greatly multiply your pain in childbearing, in pain you shall bring forth children" (Gen. 3:16). How far ought, may, must, our emancipation go from this form of suffering? The longer I reflect on the pain of birth, the more I realize that I do not want to get rid of it. That sounds odd, even masochistic. Is it possible that such insistence on the pain of the birthing woman is only one of those self-delusions, a means of transfiguring things of the past, like one's own childhood? I don't want to deny the pain or transmogrify it in an ideology of sacrifice that has the mother putting her own life at risk for the new life. Nor do I make my own those late interpretations of the biblical narrative of the fall that are hostile to women, that make the pains of childbearing a punishment for the sin of Eve. Neither sacrifice nor punishment can appropriately interpret the pain of birth and establish the mother-child relationship on a basis that is people-friendly rather than loaded with guilt feelings.

On the far side of sacrifice and punishment, those antiquated interpretive concepts, what can be said about the pain of birth that is free from the fixation on omnipotence? I only want to understand my own experience and integrate it into my life. Like all women who "had to go through it," as my grandmother put it, I know that the pain of giving birth is not the same as other physical pains familiar to me.

When I try to depict the essential difference between a toothache and labor pains, I focus on the transition from the pain of initial contractions to the pain of hard labor. The distinction between the two forms of pain is decisive for the inner experience of birthing.

The pains of initial contractions, often hours long, have something in common with the senseless toil, hardship, and exertion that the biblical narrative explains as the burden of people working the land: "Cursed is the ground because of you, in toil you shall eat of it all the days of your life" (Gen. 3:17). And yet women's experience of the hardships of pregnancy and the pains of giving birth is something different from the fruitless drudgery of working the land that is often enough robbed of its reward. In the initial contractions, pain attacks me, it makes me double over, captures me, carries me off, violates me, and makes me scream. But the heavy work of giving birth leads into a different sort of labor pain that many women, myself included, experienced as an enormous liberation.

Viktor von Weizsäcker, the great Heidelberg physician, says that "something" always hurts a patient in pain. Even when the pain reaches down into the very core of the heart, her or his illness is actually and always something "about" the patient and not she or he as such. This also applies to labor pains. Only in the transition to the pains of hard labor do the pain and I enter into a different relationship one to the other. Here the pain and I work together. The feeling of being able to do something, to help out, to go beyond the passive suffering and become a participating subject is part of the experience of happiness in giving birth. A new quality of pain is experienced, but still beneath the pains. The midwife no longer placates; she stops consoling and reassuring and now challenges, urges, commands. And the body forgets how to defend itself, forgets its self-protective mechanisms, its wish to hide somewhere—a wish often accompanied by the wish to die rather than suffer any longer.

What changes in the transition to the pain of hard labor? The pain is no smaller than before, but it becomes different because I bring it on myself. The separation between my pain and me, in which I was only a captive to pain, is over. I flex my muscles with all my strength, no longer using my inner energy defensively but proactively. Now I seek life and not protection from the enemy pain. British psychiatrist R. D. Laing critiqued the technical approach to pain in a short poem.

Take this pill.
It takes away the pain.
It takes away the Life.
You're better off without.

Like the atomic bomb, the pill is a tool that has lost its instrumental character and now rules over us. Perhaps the pain of birth is the plainest outcry against this thinking, which shuns contact, connectedness, and injury in order to make existence machinelike. The real experience of women contradicts the dreams of those who want to do away with both hard physical labor and natural childbirth. But it would be superficial to regard the opposition to the techno-model of life as merely women-specific. Such opposition has relevance for all humankind.

This archaic experience of women, moving from the pain of initial contraction to that of hard labor, seems to me to be fundamental for every relation to pain that is appropriate to human beings. The fact that this experience hardly appears even in serious philosophical reflection, such as that of Viktor von Weizsäcker, is a symptom of one of the numerous injuries patriarchy inflicts on itself. From a humanity-oriented perspective, it would seem that it is not without great cost that such experience is ignored.

Do we human beings deal with our pain only as men do? Do repulsion, defense, anesthetization—that is, the great technologies of security—really exhaust what our culture has to say about pain? Is the current response to the pain of birth that of avoiding the "birth" event itself? "It is not to happen; You're better off without it." The conception, cultivation, and delivery of genetically manipulated homunculi who—susceptible neither to cancer nor neurosis—can go on functioning even in a totally destroyed natural environment seems to be the aim.

This horrid vision of the human being made in the image of the machine cries out for resistance, for visions of life other than the predominating ones. Not only do we need different proposals of what is to be researched and developed; we also need different visions of life. Is the astronaut, packed in a space suit and hovering there weightless, an image of life? How about the woman in labor? We need to remind ourselves that there once was a time when genetic technology did not determine the beginning—and nuclear technology the end—of life. People had a different relationship with pain and with themselves. They had fashioned a language which shared and made sense of pain. Reflection on pain is perhaps most clearly pronounced in the Christian religion. I do not believe that we can abandon its language, questions, images, and reflections.

When I ask myself why the archaic pain of birth had meaning for my relation to life, what it is that I do not want to miss even though it hurts, I find that my theological expression is reduced to stammering. But stammering is a characteristic of the liveliest theologies today. What I do know is that pain is part of life because pain is part of love. I do not wish to have a God free of pain, for I could not trust such a God. The image of life I find helpful is not that of the invulnerable Siegfried who bathed in the blood of the dragon. The culture I seek is not one of domination and of having to win; it is one of compassion. The Christian religion could help people get ready for such a culture, because it derives its intensity from pain. It has interpreted the deepest pain as a pain of birth.

Again and again the New Testament uses the image of birth to tell of God's history with human beings. The pains of labor and hard work play a decisive role here. In his Epistle to the Romans, Paul describes the contemporary situation of the whole creation, as well as of those who have faith, as a birth. The pain is still present; the children of God cry out in the pains of labor and thereby engage in the work of liberation. Paul writes, "I consider that the sufferings of this present time are not worth comparing with the glory that is to be revealed to us. For the creation waits with eager longing for the revealing of the children of God. . . . We know that the whole creation had been groaning and in labor pains until now; and not only the creation, but we ourselves, who have the first fruits of the Spirit, groan inwardly while we wait for . . . the redemption of our bodies" (Rom. 8:18f and 22f NRSV).

This section has often been misunderstood because it was looked at too much from the perspective of creation as null, void, and transitory. What Paul means is actually not later interpreters' "pathos of nullity" but the reality of "hope for human beings in unbearable pain." He knew what illness, persecution, imprisonment, and torture meant. The cries and groans of a woman in labor do not signify doom and gloom; the image of birth evokes a new way of looking at struggle and transformation, a perspective experienced by women in the pangs of hard labor.

Paul even says of himself that, like a mother in the process of giving birth, he suffers pangs of birth until Christ is formed in his children (Gal. 4:19). By making the pain of women in labor his central image, Paul explains what is meant by Christian hope. The pain of women during birth is pain on behalf of life. A Christian relation to pain cannot fall below the level of what women experience in labor pains. The crying and groaning Paul speaks of refers to the last stage of giving birth; it is the labor of hope of those who in the hopelessness of "this" world wait for God. The Messiah does not come without the labor pains of messianic time.

The real question the pain of birth gives us would be how we might come to understand pain as birthing pain, labor pain as doors opening, groaning as "the onset of the glory of the freedom of God's children." How do we approach our pains so that they do not torment us like pointless kidney stones but, as pains of labor, prepare the new being? What would a theology of pain look like that does not toil away at the question of theodicy and worry about how a great and all-good God can permit bad things to happen to good people? We need a different theology of pain that finally feminizes the questions and relates our pain to the pain of God. The question then will be: How does our pain become the pain of God? How do we become part of the messianic pain of liberation, part of the groaning of a creation that is in travail? How do we come to suffer so that our suffering becomes the pain of birth?

I have been deeply moved in the last few years every time I meet people, often still very young, for whom the eradication of trees and butterflies, our sisters and brothers, as St. Francis called them, involves substantial pain. What does this pain do to those who suffer it? How does it change them? What does it want to reveal? How do we in such pain become those who are in labor and are giving birth? How do we awaken from this nightmare of having to destroy? How are we born anew?

Christian tradition pushes its knowledge of birth quite far; even death has again and again been understood as a birth. People have been so able to transform even the senseless, bitter suffering of dying that they moved from the pains of initial contraction to those of hard labor and from fighting against pain to accepting death.

We are neither machines nor beings domesticated to run the treadmill of consumerism. We are capable of suffering because we are capable of love. Activities like loving, suffering, giving birth, and dying are already a form of resistance against the imperatives of the economy under which we live. To bring children into the world and slowly to birth one's death and to accept it rather than to get it over with, quickly and if possible without awareness of it—as our shabbiest fantasies would have it—are acts of participation in creation. They refuse to fall in love with the alien reality of money and violence that has laid hold of life. The pain of birth encourages and convinces us of life. Just as a piece of bread can convince us of God, so this pain is a sacrament, a sign of God's presence. How could we ever have lost it?

THE GIFT OF TEARS

A few years ago, a younger woman in our family died of kidney disease. My husband visited her in the hospital before she died. He said this about his sister's extended time of dying, "She was all covered with tubes. The machines to which she was attached drew all attention to themselves. I would have liked to hold her hand or, when she became restless, to wipe the perspiration off her forehead. But it was impossible. I caught myself behaving very differently than I had intended. I felt compelled to keep an eye on the changing readings on the machines. I was changed from being a brother, who wanted to be with his dying sister, into a component of the dying-machine to which she was attached."

A normal death in a normal hospital in a Western country. A death without dignity, without awareness, without peace. A death that came a few hours later because a young medical professional (less and less am I able to use the word "physician") wanted to keep the process going for a few more hours. Dying is mechanized, and death has no social place anymore. Friends and relatives have no place in the process of dying. What was still a public event in a village parish and was not hidden from children has been removed for citified life and has become a taboo that one dares not break.

I do not want to have to die like my sister-in-law. I have also moved beyond the heroic, machine-driven desire to get death over and done with, bang, bang. I cherished that rather un-Christian fantasy long enough. I suspect that it is a common desire and that nothing more or better comes to mind for most people of our culture than to die quickly, noiselessly, quietly, without pain, unconsciously.

When human beings are treated long enough as components of a machine, it affects not only death but also life. Do our arrangements for dying really have to be so devoid of dignity as they are? In earlier times, prayer was offered to God for a "merciful death"; this meant that one had prepared oneself religiously for dying. It was not merely a matter of a motor shutting off, a battery running dry. What is a "merciful death"?

"Mercy" is found only when one needs it and when it is not merely a cog in a big wheel.

Knowing of and preparing oneself for death, the desire to put one's things in order, are endeavors to humanize death. Just as we can humanize our sexuality through something we call love, we can humanize dying. But to mercy belongs a conscious awareness shared with other human beings. Conscious awareness and sharing communication: how much more they are than the quick death we dream of! How wonderful it would be to live in a land where no one dies alone and in dying one's dignity is untouched.

The question of lost communication arises not only in the face of death but also afterward. Fulbert and I once attended the funeral of a friend and colleague who had died suddenly. He was not old. The day before he died we had shared a meal and made plans for our work together. He was a fine teacher, highly esteemed by the students; he stood for what he said. Our friend was an educated atheist, as was his wife. Both had left the church. Now we attended his funeral. We sat in the mortuary; the coffin stood at the front. We waited in silence for ten minutes, after which the coffin was placed in the hearse. We went to the grave; the coffin was lowered. When the last people arrived, it was already over. We stood around for a few minutes and then went home.

The hopeless silence of the funeral is a dreadful memory. Everything within us cried out: Why did our friend have to die so early? What's the point of such a death? We were full of anger and sadness, but we all kept this to ourselves. Our sadness didn't come out; it found no words, no gestures, no song, no curse; we remained silent.

The next day, there was a meeting, and the chairperson made a brief reference to our colleague's death, saying that there should be no speeches now; instead, would we rise, please, and silently remember the departed? Death had no language and no expression anymore. The meager remains of expression involved rising for a few moments, standing in embarrassment, not knowing what to do with our hands. It was a relief when the chairperson returned to the day's agenda.

But can one "return to the day's agenda" when someone dies? When important things occur in our lives, can one let go of mourning, praising, thinking, cursing, crying, accusing, praising, and honoring? What happens to us when our life becomes so mute and unceremonious? Does life itself not wither when there is no language any more for all that takes place in it?

Is it consoling to be able to cry? Is it a loss when tears come no more? I try to think about this question in relation to my own experience with being able to cry. I recall vividly a conversation I had some twenty years ago with the editor of a radio station. Almost casually he told me that in the Catholic liturgy there is a prayer for tears. I was startled, because I realized I was lacking something. Today I believe that my older friend's remark was by no means casual. Perhaps he knew me better than I knew myself and had sensed something of the sorrow that was in me. He wanted to point me to the loosening and cleansing power of tears. The point had not been to have a discussion, and our medium had not been that of psychological analysis. The issue was the ability to weep and the medium was religion. I became alarmed, because I realized that I had not wept for a long time. My alarm was the beginning of a prayer.

Not too long ago, young people in despair and full of aggression roamed the streets of Zürich; one of the graffiti they sprayed on the walls of houses was, "We already have enough reason to weep, even without your tear gas." Those words affected me deeply. When I think about weeping now and about the gift of tears, I remember not only the victims of Hiroshima who can no longer weep, I also think of the gas and how those who no longer want to weep order its use against those who "already have enough reason to weep."

It often seems to me as if there were only two languages allowed in the world: the language of science, which is free of values and void of feelings, and the language we hear daily in advertising. The latter is banal, trivializing all feelings: love is linked to a car; purity, to a detergent. Beneath this superficiality there exists the nonlanguage of sullen irritability, the feeling that one has been violated and the desire to strike back. What schools and formational institutions teach is a rational, detached language, as far removed as possible from action. It is speech from which have been removed the gestures of movement, the color of dialect, the beats of acceleration and deceleration, the rhythms and expressions of pain and joy. It is the kind of plastic language of politicians who could say of the neutron bomb only that it is really nothing different.

Feelings, fears, and joys are denied in this language and count for nothing. In it, the word "emotional" becomes an invective. How many times have I been told, "Don't be so emotional," or, "You are simply much too emotional"? In these words mistrust is palpable, feelings are un-speakable—they must not be expressed and should not actually do anything. It is as if they were stillborn. There is to be no crying in our culture and so we have let go of the purifying and consoling power that the Christian tradition has ascribed to tears.

To live without tears is to live in a culture that is poor in expression and incapable of feelings. We deny the need for the Spirit that comforts and leads into truth: We imagine that we can live without spirit, without pain made known, and without consolation. We have forgotten the prayer for the gift of tears.

While in New York, I came to know Dorothy Day, founder of the Catholic Worker movement; on account of her uncompromising Catholicism, many regarded her as a living saint. She was both pacifist and anarchist. During the Vietnam War, she took part in protest actions and was arrested once; many Christians in the United States then understood the kind of war and the kind of system it was that had to throw this utterly fearless old woman in jail. What moved me most deeply about her is something I heard only after her death. Like every human being who hungers and thirsts for justice and peace, Dorothy Day also had periods of complete exhaustion, sorrow, and pain. I was told that she would then withdraw and cry—for hours and days. She would sit there, talk to no one, eat nothing, and just cry. She did not withdraw from her struggle-filled, active life for the poorest of the poor. She never ceased to look upon war, and preparation for war, as a crime against the poor. But at certain times she wept, long and bitterly.

When I discovered this, I understood better what pacifism is, what God means in the midst of defeat, how the Spirit comforts us and leads us into truth. I understood that comfort is not had by giving up truth, that one does not happen at the expense of the other. That Dorothy Day cried for days on end means for me that the Spirit's consolation bears, at the same time, its own inconsolability. With Dorothy Day, we can learn to pray for the gift of tears.

What I also learned from this remarkable woman is that spirituality is a movement of the Spirit where separation between inward and outward—which had become so terribly complete in the religion-free funeral described earlier—is done away with. In spirituality, what is inward is to become outward, visible and audible. When we learn to share pain and joy with others, everyday life is hallowed, because our desires and fears begin to radiate in it. Our lives and experiences are not casual items to be discarded but treasures worthy of being remembered and reflected upon, lamented and named.

God is no automat, to be fed coins for delivery of what we want. The great wishes for justice, happiness, and well-being, for life worthy of a human being, are not just magically there somewhere inside us; they have to be learned. And we learn them by expressing them. The misery of the poor consists not only in their lack of bread, water, and clothes. It consists also in that loss of the great wishes for themselves, in that they can barely still imagine that life can be different.

I have experienced prayer as an intensive preparation for living, as an attempt to make God the ally against the insults and destruction heaped on the poor. Why is it so hard to pray? Why do we feel ashamed doing it and admitting that we do? There are a number of reasons. Prayer has often been misused. It certainly happens that with their prayers people mumble themselves into a state of weakness and hopelessness. But perhaps it also has something to do with the fact that our wishes and demands of life are too small.

In recent years I participated in a number of peace services that were marked by an impressive cohesiveness, rigor, and truthfulness. They shunned generic talk about and prayers for peace. They recalled how our people had already, twice in this century, supported arming the nation to the teeth. Peace was given its current name: nonviolence. By expressing our greatest wishes, we gave those wishes depth and came to understand ourselves better. The unarmed God became just a touch more visible.

How can we sing the Lord's song in a strange land? By an exodus from the Egypt of capitalism, by taking others' and our own pain seriously, and by manifesting at every level of our lives the wholeness that has become real for us in Christ. We manifest this wholeness physically and psychically, rationally and spiritually, in our toils for justice and a life that is worthy of human beings. We also show it in our lament about the defeats, in the experience of liberation. A small congregation in New York begins its eucharistic worship each Sunday by repeating, "We are here to celebrate our liberation."

When I think of worship services that have moved me the most, the following come to mind:

- The old garage in the Via Ostia in Rome, where the former Benedictine Abbot Giovanni Franzoni and his group celebrated mass. They had been driven out of the stately basilica *Fuori le muri* when they began their advocacy for the homeless. In my judgment, the occupation of that church by several thousand *senza tecco*—without shelter—was an act that lives on now, in hymn, prayer, and reflection.

• The Liturgical Night at the *Kirchentag* in Düsseldorf in 1973, when Philip Potter, then Secretary of the World Council of Churches, was invited to bring a word of greeting. He took the microphone and sang for 4,000 people the West Indian calypso "Our Father, who art in Heaven." Liturgy grows from a deep and unswerving love for the masses, it reiterates our private experiences with God, it is public and provocative—as Jesus was.

• Easter Sunday in Canaan Baptist Church in the heart of Harlem. I have never understood as I did then that liturgy is the self-expression of those present so that they become a community. Their "Amen," "Yes, Reverend," and "Hallelujah," their singing, clapping, walking about in the sanctuary, calling, crying, and moaning made that very clear to me. There were elements there of a wholeness that more often than not we experience disjointedly as art, politics, community relations, social welfare, and education. That Sunday's holistic work of art showed me what liturgy could be: a remembering that promises a future.

A TWOSOME AND IN TANDEM

It is said that marriage is a drama: Everything depends on staging. Fulbert and I like to stage our quarrels in terms of our very different origins. In the rural Roman Catholic region of Saarland, where Fulbert hails from, people would say, "The new teacher is Protestant *but* a nice person." In my family, one might hear that "The new lecturer in ancient history is Catholic *but* really intelligent."

We draw on the contrasts not only in class and denomination, but also in the customs of everyday life, the songs we sing at Christmas, and the way we try to raise children. For a quarter of a century, Fulbert has had to put up with my far too strong tea, and I with his far too strong coffee; he mocks my "Protestant fixation with truth," and I his easygoing "Catholic imprecision."

We consider marriage a desideratum insofar as it makes it easier for men and women to become human. This is a relative statement, not an abstract one; marriage is not something to be justified at any cost. It is an arrangement, a social agreement, an institution, for which reason what Jesus said about the institution of the sabbath applies also to marriage: "The sabbath was created for the sake of human beings, not human beings for the sabbath" (Mark 2:27). Marriage exists for the sake of people, and not people for the sake of marriage. Similarly, woman was not "created for marriage," as for so long we were supposed to believe. No man and no woman is created for marriage.

Martin Buber played a significant role for Fulbert and me. Before we had come to know each other, we had both visited Buber in Israel. I was a perplexed young religion teacher, on my first trip to Israel as part of Christian-Jewish cooperation. Fulbert was a Benedictine father from Maria Laach, driven by the question whether to stay or to leave. Those visits were for both of us like a secret, a gift, a well-guarded treasure. Years later, in 1966, we came to know each other at a conference of Christians and Jews in Jerusalem. When we found out what ties bound us to Martin Buber, Fulbert suggested spontaneously that we visit Buber's grave together the next day. All else had its beginning there. And the great philosopher of religion became, after his death, what in Yiddish is called a *Schadchen*, a marriage broker.

Buber's philosophy became very important in my understanding of marriage. In his *I and Thou*, he speaks of two basic relationships that constitute human life. One is the relationship of an I to a Thou, the pure and unmediated, language-transcending nearness of one to another. The other relationship is that of the I to an It, the mediated, world-oriented, creative relation to things. Love can renounce world and It, for love knows islands of pure I-Thou encounters. But it seemed to us that marriage happens exactly where the relationship of I-Thou and I-It intersect; here the world, that is, accountable and mutually determined work, comes into its own. We perceived the chances for marriage to be where there is a common field to be cultivated, even one that has not yet come into view.

The institution of marriage came into being with agriculture; it requires a third entity shared by both partners, whether it be children or, as with Brecht and Weigel, a theater. Without commonality in work and without common social goals, there is no marriage; without a vision of the other life, there is no marriage, only the mere and dull consumerist orientation of two persons. Without the It, there is no I-Thou; without the world, there can be no common growing. One of my best-known books is *Im Hause des Menschenfressers* (*Of Love and War*); it is dedicated to my marriage partner.

FOR FULBERT

Imbiber and diluter
first and last reader
father confessor in resistance

one who knows the night
and lights candles
to read the book

he protects me
from others and from myself
and gives up on no one

except himself at times

compañero

In our conversations, we found again and again that another condition for marriage is friendship. When Elke, one of our friends, was married, her husband said to her, "You put an end now to you and your women friends; now that you have me, you don't need a woman friend." In this prohibition of other relationships, the wide range of human eroticism is channeled into one instance. Marriage, thus reified and reduced to the bedroom, brutally prohibits friendship, and the relationship becomes obsessive. What is a community of life becomes a consumptible, and what should be the intersection of diverse and numerous interests and activities becomes an isolated, asocial point of fixation. A marriage without common work, without common joy, without shared vision suffocates in its own restrictedness.

In one of Bertolt Brecht's stories, a woman is asked about her husband. She gives this reply: "I lived with him for twenty years. We slept in the same room and the same bed. We ate our meals together. He told me all about his business dealings. I was acquainted with his parents and socialized with all his friends. I knew of all his illnesses, even those he wasn't aware of. Of all who knew him, I knew him best." The decisive word to describe this woman's relationship to her husband is "to know." She knows everything, and that means she is in control. For her, "being in the know" serves that control. Actually, we can know only something that is dead, an object. With what lives, we can only have experiences, and grow to be more and more engaged with it. "To know" is part of the domain of I-It relationships, the domain that with its sheer weight and routine makes many a marriage unbearable. Fulbert and I were spared this particular life-threatening crisis, but not others. I tried to express such thoughts in another poem written for him:

> When you are engulfed by grief
> I would like to live in our tree house like we used to
> sleep in your tent and share
> the rain and noise that settled over us
> It was good to know
> long ago
> what is yours is mine
> I dared not open your door yesterday
> full of worry
> I watch your senseless pain
> Standing at the sideline

I have become a hawk
watching your every move
You drink more and more
I become more and more sober from your drinking

When you are engulfed by grief
I want your time and mine to be at one
but I am much older
and smile
when I brush your forehead
and know better what is good for you
But I am much younger and ask you
like all women ask their husbands
must you always go there?
must you give her everything of your grief?

When you are engulfed by grief
it is there I want to live even when we are not at one
Am I to have my weapons wrested from my hands
just because you let them fall from yours
Can I be for you
other than by fighting against you
and begging you to come along
into another land beloved brother

When you are engulfed by grief
I do not want to watch
I do not want to be older
I do not want to be younger
I do not want to remain sober
I would like to live in our tree house
when you are engulfed by grief

AN UMBRELLA CALLED CHURCH

I was not born into the world of the church. I cannot consider myself deformed or neuroticized by the church. The policeman-god who checks under the bedcovers is known to me only from reports of people whom the church has damaged. I have never been employed by the church or received remuneration from it. The fact of this biographical distance from it has freed me for critique and affirmation, for anger *and* love. To put it concretely: It has freed me to distinguish between the church from above and the church from below. Beside the power-monger Pope Innocent III, I always saw the *poverello* Francis. The distinction between tendencies toward oppression and toward liberation in the history of Christianity is a hermeneutical principle that has pervaded my entire being.

For example, in relation to the Christian church's role in the First World War, I feel alienation, disgust, repugnance, and shame. I often look upon the empirical church as a structure "from above" that, in alliance with money and military power, again and again betrays its own truth. In a biblical image, the church is often like Judas, who delivered Christ to the established religious authorities. Or is it more like the male disciples who, discouraged and defeated, left Jesus alone and fled? And then there are times when the thought overtakes me that the church is like Peter, who denied that he had ever known anything at all about peace and justice. Very rarely do I see the church, like him, weeping bitter tears.

My theology never conformed to the church. I wanted to write "edifying discourses" like Kierkegaard's. Presumably, my readership to a large extent consists of people who have been alienated from the church and who for good reasons no longer attend its services. Often they switch their support to Amnesty International, but still sense that there is something missing in their nonreligious endeavors. They look for and need something different. These are the people whose language I speak.

I seek to find out how we can "love God above all things." Precisely for the sake of this search, it seemed necessary to me to break with certain traditional teachings or religious assurances void of serious thought. An example of such is the acceptance of supernatural events as true, or believing in an existence after death. Bonhoeffer's insistence on the "radical this-worldliness of Christianity" helped me here. Later, reading the mystics, I repeatedly found references to this atheism that faith requires. In conversations with humanist or socialist atheists, I often found myself saying, "Well, my friends, we Christians have long been as atheistic as you are." The differences emerged when we spoke of the bread of hope and where it is to be found. They were about the spirituality that I was looking for.

But this spirituality requires an incarnation; it needs an institution that passes on language and sacred texts, images and signs, rituals and sacraments. In my view, it is a postmodern mistake to think that without traditions we are freer. What is new in our situation is that traditions can no longer be forced upon anyone. The fact that authoritarian religion is dying before our eyes does not say anything about other, quite different forms and possibilities of religion and church. Perhaps the church is not so much the crumbling edifice we see but more a tent for the wandering people of God. The tent is not always where I am, but ultimately I keep meeting the tent-people—on the street, among the homeless, or in the courts. Unlike the church, the holy is much more an encounter than it is a structure, fixed or movable.

A friend of mine, the American Jesuit and resister Daniel Berrigan, once spoke of the church as "an umbrella." It protects us from the cold rain; sometimes it opens too slowly and we get rained on. Often it is not very efficient. Still, it is there, Dan said, and I would not want to do without it.

Many years after the conversation we had during a demonstration at the Pentagon, this image came back to me. It was at the time of the bloodless revolution in the former German Democratic Republic. There, too, the church had often been an inefficient shelter for many people in the movement for citizens' rights. On occasion, it left people out in the rain. Nevertheless, in 1989 I was proud of our paltry umbrella. After all, for the first time in 400 years, the Protestant church stood on the side of the people.

This nice picture must not minimize the difficulties and conflicts that I had, again and again, with the official church. But I never lost sight of this double image of hate, ignorance, and ill will on the one hand, and openness, readiness to learn and change on the other. For that I thank God.

It almost seems that my life has been staged so that the huge fights and mean-spirited attacks that occurred regularly always brought me new friends and allies. Among them was the friend and biographer of Dietrich Bonhoeffer, Eberhard Bethge. The president of the Rhenish Synod in Germany once said some awful things about me; his precise words I cannot recall. What I do remember is the large bouquet of flowers Eberhard Bethge sent, even though I did not know him at that time. In a manner of speaking, he apologized for the Synod, for these men; he was plainly ashamed. This action provided the foundation for a friendship with the Bethges.

Eberhard Bethge's passion for life allowed him no academy-like theological self-censorship. Being very unclerical and very musical, Bethge was free enough to make it known when he was angry about something. He did not have to become a leftist—whatever that may mean—in order to do so. All he needed to do was to stand, obstinately, conservatively, where the New Testament had put him. And that was in a society that ever so quickly forgot and suppressed its immediate past. It was rushing to the right, so that suddenly more and more Christians felt pushed into the subversive corner where "resistance" became no mere historical subject.

When the Political Evensong was anathematized by the Roman Catholic chancery in Cologne, and attacked by the Protestant governing body, Heinrich Böll called this a perfidious ecumenism. At that time, Eberhard Bethge was a member of that Protestant body, but he was not among those who maintained that faith and politics have nothing to do with each other. Nor was he one to hide with others behind specious differentiations, that is, that the ideas of those responsible for the Evensong were not developed fully enough to be seriously discussed. This is not to say that in relation to the Evensong he was one with us. But he did invite us and a certain number of ministers from the Rhenish Church region to his study center at Rengsdorf. Here we could learn and study together, and Bethge himself would take part in the discussion. Rengsdorf was a place where we did not feel watched and we learned from his critique. It seemed to us that Bethge was simply less afraid. And he had no need to make others feel afraid.

To a certain extent, the campaigns against me climaxed when, in 1983, I delivered one of the plenary addresses at the sixth assembly of the World Council of Churches in Vancouver. I was to speak on "life in its fulness." Even the invitation was met with very vehement protest on the part of the German Protestant Church (EKD) and, particularly, the evangelicals. But Bärbel von Wartenberg, at that time at the Women's Desk of the

WCC in Geneva, and her husband, Philip Potter, the black General Secretary from Jamaica, upheld the invitation.

The reasons for those protests were purely personal. For more than thirty years, the evangelicals have portrayed me as a witch who should really be burned at the stake. In the circles of the right-wing movement "No Other Gospel," one could often hear the pun on my name, which rhymes with the German word for hell, *Hölle*: "Go to Sölle and descend to hell," or "Descended into Sölle." In such expressions, political and sexist objections were fusing themselves with the rejection of a radical theology that relied on biblical criticism.

I had expected little else from the evangelicals, but I was surprised by the reaction of the Protestant church's council in Hannover. It declared that the World Council of Churches' decision was "very troubling," that I was not representative of, and could not speak for, the Christians of West Germany. It was not clear to me how they could know this for sure. I think that I did speak for a wide range of Christians. The idea that any higher-ranking church official represents the entire spectrum seems quite un-Protestant to me and more in the style of talk-show hosts. When you are very superficial and have little to say, it is easy to think that one is actually speaking for many people. Claims of being more representative generally mean less substance.

There is a certain quality of hatred that I came to feel every time the press had once again quoted one and a half sentences of mine. And so it was in Vancouver. The first sentence of my address read as follows: "Dear sisters and brothers, I speak to you as a woman from one of the richest countries of the earth, a country with a bloody history that reeks of gas, a history some of us Germans have not been able to forget; I come from a country that today holds the greatest concentration of atomic weapons in the world, ready for use." That sentence reaped abuse against me for weeks on end. But I had spoken it deliberately because I wanted to make it clear in an international gathering that I come from Germany and I know what that means. Without explaining at length, time being of the essence, I wanted to signal that I am not done with that history. Some of us cannot forget it.

In the Federal Republic of Germany, this was the only sentence that was quoted, and the reaction was swift: "How dare you foul the nest—why don't you go to East Germany?" And this was *mild* invective. A storm of indignation blew up in West Germany over this one sentence, but the people from developing countries understood me very well.

The question of peace was what their anger was all about. I was unhappy with the West German church, which I experienced as one of the richest and least prophetic churches in existence. Its waffling on the issue of peace made it unique in the '80s. Neither the Dutch churches nor the Christians of East Germany, not to speak of the Catholic bishops in the U.S., issued statements of such obeisance and subservience to the state. It weighed heavily on me that efforts to engender a little more courage and devotion to peace within the West German church had still not met with success. That church could not state plainly, as the Dutch had done, that the possession of nuclear weapons is a sin, that first use of those weapons is to be condemned, and that even the threat to do so is incompatible with faith in redemption. Instead we got peace rhetoric that was vague and unclear. For decades the EKD hobbled along, far behind in the debate on peace. This was reflected in its relationship to the World Council of Churches.

Next to the laundry basket of hate mail, there were very fine letters of solidarity, particularly from women. Often signed by twenty or thirty women, these letters asked of the EKD offices in Hannover, "Why is this woman not representative? She certainly represents us. Most likely we would no longer be believers had we not read or heard things by Dorothee Sölle."

Now I feel much less alone in the church than I did some years ago. Have I perhaps become milder and more toothless? I do not think so. The movement called the Conciliar Process names the subjects that occupy the center of Christian faith at the end of the millennium. They are justice, peace, and the integrity of creation. This momentum and its orientation carry me along, oriented toward reconciliation. My hope is for an end to the war between rich and poor that has shed and still sheds more blood than we can measure, and to the war between all of us and the earth who bears us. In this process I feel at home and borne by Christian tradition.

In the course of interviews with journalists over the last few years about peace or the Conciliar Process, I have found positive echoes to what I understand faith and hope to be. Only to verify what they had heard, they would ask: "But you do not really mean the church when you talk like this?" Somewhat intimidated, I would reply: "Yes indeed, that is how I imagine the church, and occasionally, that is how I experience it. That is how I wish it to be—and I have a high view of the power of wishing." Using the language of religion, I pray that this is what the church might be. For in the heavy rains of today's world and its reality it helps to have "an umbrella."

The majority of Germans today no longer believe in God. Thus far, this fact did not bother me very much, because what they believed in earlier I could not necessarily regard as God. But I am concerned about this statistic for another reason; I fear that the stance is mutual. What reason could God have to believe in us?

MUTUALITY

Someone once asked Sigmund Freud what the healthy, unneurotic human being we all want to be really looks like. Freud is supposed to have replied that this human being is able to work and to love. I took up this basic idea in a theology of creation and wrote a book that draws conclusions from my experiences of both loving and working.

Surely it is one of my life's greatest privileges that I can fill my work with meaning, that it has to do with what I desire. A criterion of good work is that it must be an expression of the worker's self. Another aspect of meaningful work is relatedness to other human beings, an accountability to society. We desire to produce what others need. For this author it means that her work is to be not only an expression of herself but that it creates community.

I'm happy, therefore, that there are people who need my work. I receive numerous letters from people—often just to thank me, saying that something I had written helped them. Their responses let me experience my work as beautiful. The most lovely echo is in a short letter I received recently: "Dear Ms. Sölle! I am psychologically challenged. But over the course of the years, I have found things in your books that have helped me in never entirely losing faith in my much trampled-on human dignity. This Christmas I finally want to thank you for that."

An American friend of mine, feminist theologian Carter Heyward, has helped me a lot toward a better understanding of resonance. She became involved in public conflict with her institution when, in the '70s, she and ten other women were ordained priests in the Anglican church—a first in that church's history. I came to know her shortly thereafter; I had heard much about her already and had read her book, *A Priest Forever*. I was not pleased about her ordination, and, three minutes after meeting her, asked her why in God's name she would want to be a priest. Are we not all priests, with or without ordination? Did she not believe in the priesthood of all believers? A passionate debate between us ensued.

From this dispute a wonderful friendship developed. In her church and in her scholarly addresses, I heard Carter sing liturgical pieces. Her singing made it clearer than words ever could what power there is in tradition. I shared with her my feeling that we need more than rational discourse and we need to experiment with different forms of communication. We met each other not only in New York and Boston, where Carter teaches, but also in Nicaragua, where we traveled as international observers of an election. With tears we shared the bitterness of the electoral defeat of the Sandinista revolution.

Mutuality is one of the most important concepts Carter has worked through and developed theologically; above all, she lives it in her conduct. But it was in conversations with her and her longtime friend Beverly Harrison that I began to realize how much real relationships are based in mutuality, needing and being needed by another. Nobody lives alone; everyone is sustained by others. I do not just give; for when I truly give I also take. Giving and taking are actually *one* performance for which, oddly enough, we always employ two words.

I can give something to you only when you take it, or when you give me something. Therein lies a very deep mutuality. I can say something to you only when you listen. I can respond only to what you ask me about. I am sustained by the letters I receive from desperate people, prisoners, refugees, or advocates for harassed Turkish families in Germany, asking me to help or requesting specific action. These are not simply burdens but also tasks that strengthen me; I experience them not only as a demand but also as a gift.

The request somebody utters is perhaps one of the greatest gifts one can receive in life. It is not only that something is to be done. It's also that one may be something to someone else. North American feminists use a lovely expression, "the web of life." In the early '80s, some of these North American feminists contributed to a book titled *Reweaving the Web of Life*. I often feel that the web of life carries me, all those many threads that stretch among women in particular, but also among men and women. Even though I sometimes felt miserably lost in West Germany, I always felt at home among those who have a part in this process of reweaving.

According to a basic assertion of feminist theology, God is no absolute sovereign who, independent of us, decides and governs. The creator of heaven and earth also needs us, is dependent on us; as every form of life, so God too is interdependant.

HUNGER AFTER LIBERATION

I think that today I would no longer define my theological position as "political theology." The concept had been fraught with difficulty from the outset because it had been coined by one of the Nazis' spiritual fathers, the philospher of jurisprudence, Carl Schmitt. The meaning he ascribed to this concept was a justification of the conditions existing at the time. "Every leadership needs political theology," was a very interesting and insidious conception. It meant that there just had to be incense, flags, military music, and national symbols. This sort of false state-religiosity is "political theology" in its worst sense.

Even when the concept of "political theology" began to be filled with new meaning years ago, it still lacked clarity. The new meaning was provided chiefly by Johann Baptist Metz, Jürgen Moltmann, and me, in our works *Theology of the World*, *Theology of Hope*, and *Political Theology*. In discussion with our "fathers"—Metz with Karl Rahner, Moltmann with Ernst Bloch, and I with Rudolf Bultmann—the three of us, independently, gained comparable insights. But the decision behind them that would clarify the concept of "political theology" was not yet fixed in our minds.

Today I am overwhelmed and grateful that the "theology of liberation," which first came into being in Latin America, has opened up theological dimensions that are so different from those I knew. I refer to the rereading of the Bible from the perspective of developing countries. I remember exactly the day when someone told me something about the *teología de liberación* and what I felt that day. It often happens that one has long searched for a more adequate term, and suddenly, someone utters it, hitting the nail right on the head.

In liberation theology, what comes first is praxis: the dispute, struggle, and resistance. Theology, reflection on praxis, is a necessary second step. The experiences we had in the praxis of our Political Evensong were very important to me. Here a group of Christian women and men had sought in the alternating pattern of political discussion and contemplation, struggle and prayer, to fashion together a living faith.

I understand the gospel as an instruction in struggle and contemplation, in *lutte et contemplation*, as the Prior of Taizé, Roger Schutz, puts it. I also find this quality where the New Testament presents Jesus saying: "I send you like sheep among the wolves." The disciples lived among wolves, in a realm of terror in which anyone who took even the smallest step toward justice risked life and limb. The women and men who followed Jesus knew this. Any understanding of their entire movement fails if it does not see that this was a movement of resistance against those who were intent on preventing them from doing God's will.

God's message is unambiguous: "You are to feed the hungry, clothe the naked, bury the dead, visit the imprisoned." All of these works are "forbidden" by the economic structure in which we live. It is designed to let the hungry starve, make the rich richer and the poor poorer. We live in a world where we cannot love God's creation but must destroy it. We cannot love justice. We must support the World Bank and the International Monetary Fund—the very ones who increase pauperization and have on their conscience those who have died of hunger.

Liberation theology taught me to understand the Bible not only as a summons to do God's will in a world of injustice, but also as a summons to endure discrimination, difficulties, and—certainly in many places in developing countries—martyrdom. "They who want to save their life shall lose it" means to take the risk of resistance in full awareness. Some older friends, like Eberhard Bethge, who had been a part of the resistance against the Nazis, asked critically whether that statement was still valid today, whether it was not pushing things too far. Having thought about it with many friends, I have come to believe that it is valid for us. The ways our foundations for life are being destroyed, the poor abandoned to die, and a so-called peace erected on the rule of madness, call for resistance. Becoming a Christian, growing into Christ seems possible only as one grows into a movement of resistance.

Liberation theology repeats again and again that the poor are the teachers. It sounds crazy, because we imagine that we are the great teachers and exporters of well-being, bringing medicine, technology, clean water, hygiene, and so forth to the poor. In the realm of the spiritual, there is so very much more we can learn from the poor, from their ability to hope, to begin anew, to make another attempt. We middle-class people are so easily discouraged. We sustain two or three setbacks, fail to arrive where we had planned to be, or are prevented here or there from publishing or speaking, and everything seems pointless. Here I am speaking about my own experiences. That discouragement is weakness; it is the cynicism growing among us. Often engaged in much more extensive struggles, and holding out even though the objective prospects are so much smaller, the poor know exactly where their strengths lie. They keep up their struggle.

Knowing that weapons and money are not the only rulers of this world justifies us in also having hope. When we withdraw into our private domain, however, and imagine that only as a private individual can one save oneself, we destroy ourselves. Withdrawing from public engagement for the sake of privacy, or surrounding or busying ourselves with beautiful things and creating a cultured life in the midst of the barbarism we live in, is to lose life. Because what is at stake is not our cultured little island but the liberation of the whole people of God, first and foremost, the liberation of the poor.

To illustrate what liberation theology means, let me name some particular people. One is Oscar Romero, the murdered archbishop of San Salvador. From him we may learn that the dead are not dead. He is more alive than ever; it was impossible to kill him. A North American folk song about the revolutionary labor leader Joe Hill proclaims: "What they forgot to kill went on to organize." That is true also for Oscar Romero. He draws us into a big conversion process where the poor and the uneducated are the ones who help the rich and those with academic credentials become converted. Through his death, Romero, himself having been converted through the death of a friend (Jesuit priest Rutilo Grande), also converts us and many others who for so long refused to accept this reality: the dead are not dead—not Romero, not the sixty thousand whose lives were taken in this allegedly "low intensity" war. They are not forgotten; even among us, memory is not easily extinguished.

Similarly, we are not alone, severed from the root that bears us. In saying these words, I want to say what has been said long ago, and much more clearly, by the people of El Salvador. They have already declared their Bishop Oscar Arnulfo Romero a saint. Some day the Vatican will also take notice and follow suit, but the people have taken the lead in this matter, calling him a saint, a comforter, and a helper. They call upon him. I want to help spread among us this ability to call on someone like that and to witness to the truth of another human being.

Romero became a witness in Agulares, in 1977, when Rutilo Grande was murdered; he became a witness against his clerical education and conservative predisposition. He broke with the class that had allied itself with the church. He did so slowly, without turning his back on persons in the oligarchy. But he gave up looking at the world from their perspective, and that was enough. Shortly before his death, he charged the soldiers and police: "Stop the murder! God's command says: You must not kill!" His witness was full and complete.

A silly notion exists among us that saints are completely different from us, that they are there to be looked upon in wonderment, to be prayed to or ridiculed—which amounts to the same thing. They are on a level, so the notion goes, that we can never reach. Does this fit Oscar Romero? He was by no means a model human being; like everyone else, he made mistakes. Once he visited a place where a number of people had been murdered. He made a speech, but the people became upset and tore the microphone from his hands. At first he had no idea of what he had done wrong. What the people could not tolerate was that he had not mentioned the names of the murderers. That is how the people educated Oscar Romero.

Another story has moved me even more because it is so human. The archbishop had to pay a visit to a remote, hard-to-reach village. After trekking for four hours on a muddy path, he arrived, totally exhausted, and asked for something to eat. The people gave him a small tamale; he ate it and then asked for more. Upon learning there was no more, Romero asked the villagers for forgiveness; I think he was ashamed. Oscar Romero lives, he is *presente*, as the people call out in the streets in El Salvador. As the poor draw strength from that phrase, we who are impoverished in mind and spirit may also do so. Whenever we believe that the dead are dead and that's that, we are feeding a little death within us. The murder of Oscar Romero must be "celebrated" because it signifies remembering (the juxtaposition of past [remembering] and future is deliberate).

I also learned much from another liberation theologian, Leonardo Boff. In May 1992, he was in Hamburg to deliver an address, and we exchanged a few words. I rejoiced in the clarity of his address, but I sensed that he preferred not to talk about his conflict with Rome. In retrospect, I am now aware that I was afraid. For him? For all of us? For our mother, the church?

Soon thereafter we heard the news that he had left the priesthood and his order. My distress was deeper than I could have anticipated. Leonardo leaves—what about us? Who remains at all and who remains unscathed? I called a number of friends and told them that this was a blow to Christ's whole church. Someone corrected me: "Only for the Catholic church."

Becoming annoyed, I said: "Don't talk nonsense. It's a blow to all of us, because we shall all miss him." With the deterioration of the gospel into individualism, we shall miss Leonardo Boff in the conflicts with power that are regularly imposed on us. We shall miss his spirit, his freedom, his chutzpah. We all have too little of those.

That night I wept. I often experienced liberation theology as a reformation in Europe. A different social class had the say, the mute began to speak, arbitrarily imposed power structures began to be abandoned, a new piety with new songs and prayers came into being, the Bible was being discovered by and for the poor.

A new theological thinking accompanies this *ecclesia semper reformanda*. Do we have to give up hope for a church of sisters and brothers that orients itself not by Roman law but by the gospel of the poor? Will the distorted face of the church once again become more believable? Is the institution going to shed with shame its suicidal masculinist fixation and finally come to understand power as mutual service and power-sharing?

Then I read Leonardo Boff's open letter to the "companions on the way." Perhaps my feelings of increased contradiction were the beginning of consolation. I needed to name my fears more precisely; they have to do with the frightening impression I often have and which is expressed in the image of rats leaving a sinking ship.

Of course, I was seeing this from the perspective of the rich world, or more accurately, from that of its Christian minorities. Among us there is now a massive new rush into secularity, most likely associated with the breakdown of the Communist bloc. In terms of the economy, this rush signifies that now advanced capitalism has no need any more of the lubricant of religion, or, at least, it no longer orders it from the old suppliers of religion. As far as ethics and religion are concerned, the Christian church's unbelievability is beyond measure. A European theology of liberation, which we in the minorities of the Conciliar Process were looking for, is constantly circumscribed by the power of the ecclesiastical apparatus on the one hand and, on the other, a creeping secularization, a departure, without cost or pain, from the church. The free space where we can live, celebrate, and think about liberation is becoming smaller.

But this is not the whole truth. There was another, ineradicable script in Leonardo's letter. I could call it his mystical love of the church. It is true that I often wondered about his humility. I am an impatient woman, capable of anger. But perhaps I had not seen clearly enough that he had actually gone to the limits of self-giving, and then obeyed God more than humans. For he did not turn his back on the struggle or on love, if that is at all possible. I noticed how ecumenism from below was flourishing in many places on the margins of the institutional church.

The struggle continues, Leonardo Boff said, and ecclesiastical authorities or other foes of liberation cannot take anything from us, not the Bible, not God's blessing, not Saint Francis. What reason could he have had not to celebrate the Eucharist with the *niños de la rua*, the Brazilian street-kids he cares for?

Of course, it was a fracture in his life. But the real ship of God does not sink, and it does not sail where our spellbound gaze is fixed. We still spend too much energy on the liberation of the unbelievable institution, instead of quietly carrying forward God's peace, consistently, subversively, and outside our walls. No, Leonardo Boff will not be missing; in many places of our small planet, we shall go on praying and working together. We will not lose one another: that is how I understood his letter.

I gave him a sisterly hug and remembered that Christ was also "outside the gate" and that we are to "go forth to him outside the camp" (Heb. 13:13). His peace would also be with Leonardo.

The tradition that joins us together is justice. "God is the universe," "God is the maker of the cosmos," "God is energy," "God is the light"—I can say all that, too. But, coming from the Judeo-Christian tradition, I must say first: God is justice. To know God means to do justice. This discernment does not arise from deep reflection, psychology, or cosmology. I believe that we deny our own tradition when we divert from the Jewish and Christian tradition of liberation to something different. In the West, or the First World, all Christian theology seems to have reached an end. The truly new impulses of Christianity come from very different places, for example, from the slums somewhere in Brazil. The Christianity that is alive sings new songs, prays new prayers, reads the Bible differently, and celebrates in a different fashion. Having done away with the hierarchy, the base-communities have created new cultural forms. They were born in the shortage of priests, and they discovered the priesthood of all believers.

We have every reason to learn from the Christian women and men in developing countries. Of course, our situation is quite different. We kill indirectly, and we steal the bread of the poor indirectly. Not until one understands murder by omission, or theft in terms of unjust prices for primary resources, does one recognize that we do steal from the poor and kill them. Our primary sins are sins of omission: silence, acquiescence, nodding our heads, being obedient. We sin by allowing anything and everything to be done with us.

If one finally understands what is really going on, one cannot live with a clear conscience in this bourgeois world, pursuing one's career and one's entertainment. Other priorities arise in one's life. These priorities are encompassed in the comprehensive word "resistance." The process that embodies such new priorities is the "Conciliar Process for justice, peace, and the integrity of creation." Many congregations and communities have taken up this process and they work for peace—not the phantom peace that rests on the balance of terror, the exploitation of resources, and human cunning, but for real peace, for disarmament. They work for justice, for a different ordering of the world's economy that will not let the poor be further impoverished, for industrial conversion and the protection of creation. Since the mid-'80s I have heard in this process the call to turn back, the call for a theology of liberation for the First World.

I became especially involved in Argentina. This came about in part because of Elisabeth Käsemann, daughter of my teacher, Ernst Käsemann. While in Argentina, Elisabeth disappeared one day without a trace, one of that country's victims. I can think of only one reason for her disappearance; she informed poor girls in a dairy factory of their trade-union rights. It is not that Argentinian law is all that bad; it has an old union movement. Yet Elisabeth Käsemann informed those girls of their rights, something nobody had done for them before. This was enough to bring about her being named a subversive, causing her disappearance, torture, and eventual murder. This case was a pointed lesson in why our struggle and our solidarity must also be with and for those who live under such horrible conditions.

Latin America is especially close to my heart for several reasons. With others, I worked there to publicize human rights violations in the days of military dictatorships. One of my daughters lives and works as a physician in Bolivia. One of my books, *Gott im Müll* (literally *God in the Garbage,* published as *Stations of the Cross*) is dedicated to her:

> For Caroline in Carabuco
> who does much
> that I can only dream of
> and lives things
> while I drag behind, draped in words
> she suffers things

from which I would like to have protected her
gone to shores far away and yet closer
to the memory of the fire
we all need for life
daughters and mothers

And Latin America is also a Christian continent that has given me
anew the language of my tradition. I read the same psalms as the people
there. I also dream their dream.

"WE CAN ALREADY SEE THE LIGHTS"

My love for Nicaragua has a long history. To recall it means first of all to think of the marvelous messenger who for thirty years has sent thoughts and poems, utopias and dreams, books and money back and forth—the publisher from Wuppertal, Hermann Schulz. I like to think of his publishing house, Peter Hammer Verlag, as an importer of hope and other flowers. To this day, their motto is "optimism in place of intimidation."

In 1966, Schulz introduced me to a new author, a Trappist monk and priest, the poet Ernesto Cardenal, regarded as one of the most important poets of the sixth continent. Within a few years, his poetic renderings of psalms became the bestseller of a new generation all over Latin America.

I came to know Nicaragua through its poetry, this small country in Central America whose social and political structures were shaped by oppression and neocolonialism. It was a country where landless peasants sank more and more into misery while the affluence of the feudal upper classes steadily increased, fed by foreign investment. In his poetry, in his psalms, Cardenal avoided speaking of the upper class in these words; he simply identified them as "they." He spoke of "their" leaders and feasts, "their" radio broadcasts and slogans, "their" shares and accounts.

He knew what he was talking about. Belonging to one of the oldest patrician families of Nicaragua, he was born in 1925 in the provincial town of Granada. He studied literature in Mexico and the United States. At the end of the '40s, he wrote a dissertation at Columbia University, on the modern lyrical poetry of his country.

That was the end of the smooth development of his life. His first compositions already had explosive content. In 1952 an anonymous handbill containing a political program made its way throughout Nicaragua. The underground movement broadcast the poem from all its radio stations, and it was on everyone's lips.

In April 1954, police uncovered a conspiracy in which nearly all young intellectuals of the country were involved. Cardenal was able to escape; he was already in hiding for a long time. Then came a major turning point in his life; he exchanged the barricades for the monastery. He turned his back on politics and entered the Trappist monastery, Gethsemani, in Kentucky. He was the novice of the poet-monk, Thomas Merton, himself an important interpreter of recent Latin American literature. When Merton died accidentally in 1968 in Thailand, Cardenal composed a great poem on the death of his friend, similar to the one he wrote on the death of Marilyn Monroe.

Cardenal suffered under the harsh climate of Kentucky; he hardly wrote at all, worked on sculptures, and devoted himself more and more to deep meditation. He spent a few years in a Benedictine monastery in Mexico, descending into an ever deepening silence. Yet this monastery was also "too beautiful, too luxurious" for him. He went to a monastery in Colombia, "at the end of the world," close to the jungle, in a place where dire poverty reigned, as far away as possible from civilization.

After living in monasteries for ten years, Cardenal returned to Nicaragua and settled in the village of Solentiname, on one of the islands in Gran Lago. With a few companions, he tried something new there. He wanted to establish a Trappist hermitage in order to help the peasants of Nicaragua. A modest medical polyclinic and an elementary school were the beginning of this new kind of "Christian mission." This is also where the renowned volume *The Gospel in Solentiname* came into being, one of the publications that has opened the Bible to me better than many a learned commentary.

Nicaraguan President Somoza had the little houses in Solentiname destroyed in 1977. The same year, Cardenal officially joined the Sandinistas. After their triumph in 1979, he served as Nicaragua's Minister of Culture until 1986. He represented his country at one of the Bertrand Russell Tribunals on human rights violations. He caused workshops for poets to be established among the campesinos in the countryside—the happiest times he probably spent in the otherwise not heartily embraced position of minister. On one of my sojourns in Managua, I lived in Cardenal's house, initially in his absence.

LA CASA DE ERNESTO CARDENAL

The house has stillness
    even when the TV drones
    and the rain plays drum on the garage roof at night
    or the chickens bustle into the room shrieking
Your house has stillness

The house is full of tenderness
   even when I lie awake waiting
   for someone to come to welcome me
   and I double over for loneliness in my hammock
Your house is full of tenderness

The house consoles me
   even though it does not lift my fear
   that tomorrow they will start their war
   who today try out torture-machines
Your house consoles me

The house harbors the book
   that says blessed are
   those that choose poverty
   the party of the impoverished
Your house harbors me

The house hides something
   like all houses of love
   as if the rocking chairs
   and the stones of the inner courtyard
   could reveal a secret
that I do not know Ernesto
but need to live by

   I had visited him once in Solentiname; that is where I perhaps
understood best his decision for the revolutionary struggle for liberation. An important document of that time on the question of peace in
the mind of Christians is the correspondence between Daniel Berrigan
and Ernesto Cardenal on the latter's active participation in Nicaragua's
liberation movement. Cardenal had changed his mind and moved from
a position of nonviolence to embark on the liberative struggle. Daniel
Berrigan, Jesuit and poet, himself a resistance fighter like his friend
Ernesto, asked how Cardenal could give up the principle of nonviolence
and take up the gun. "Do you not know that all who do violence not
only kill their victims but also destroy themselves?" Both men are my
friends; I never doubted their engagement and their love for God. Both
embodied something of the mystical and revolutionary spirit I consider
so necessary.

When I met Ernesto in 1979—he was in exile then—he told me that he could not respond to Dan because he loved him too much. "But you know," he added, "he does not know what revolution is." Cardenal's psalms helped me find my voice. They smoothly integrate biblical and contemporary moments. The means with which people today are threatened have changed, but fear and protest, suffering from injustice, and the jubilation over liberation have stayed the same. Cardenal did not simply "translate" psalms, as if something from the past had to be transported into the present in order to become understandable and palatable. The direction of this poetry is the opposite: Cardenal seeks to articulate what is present, and elements of biblical imagery and language offer themselves to him for that purpose. He speaks of God in a strikingly self-evident manner that sometimes even seems naive. Cardenal experiences God's absence concretely as the helplessness of human beings. As in the Psalms of old, doubt and faith are in balance—not in an intellectual sense, but existentially, as an arc from despair to hope along which the supplicant moves. For that reason, the recurring question is when God will finally intervene.

> How long, Lord, will you stay neutral?
> How long will you look on with sympathy?
> Release me from the chambers of torture and free
>   me from the concentration camp.
> Their propaganda does not serve peace but provokes war.
> You hear their radios and see their TV broadcasts.
> Do not keep silent! Awake! Arouse yourself—my God—
>   to stand with me, to defend me.

There is no place in these psalms where religion could turn into the opiate of the people. Nothing diverts the focus to something later, above, beyond. Nowhere is there consolation that would make the consoled unfaithful to the earth. For it is part of worldliness, understood—as it is here—in the Jewish and Christian sense, to enter into solidarity with all who are denied their rights, to cry out with all who suffer. It is not the presumption of the living when Cardenal dares to speak of those murdered in Auschwitz as "we," when he includes himself in "God's people of Auschwitz." To a distant observer of world history and poetry, this may appear as an all-too-chummy familiarity with the dead, as a flattering of their unique suffering. But the category of solidarity that makes itself heard here cannot be historically substantiated, empirically demonstrated, and racially or ethnically rooted. It is a mystical category, in the strict sense of the word: The solidarity of suffering is grasped in and by faith.

The "change" in Nicaragua, the electoral unseating of the Sandinistas, and the World Bank-driven pauperization of the majority have not dashed this poet's courage or silenced his voice. His great *Canto Cosmico,* a cosmic hymn of the beginning, combining myth, mysticism, and natural science, represents a new poetic departure. I wrote Ernesto a letter:

> Ernesto, when I read your poems anew, an old myth of the Western world came to mind, the story of Paris's choice. You remember the handsome young man from Troy who watches his father's flocks on Mount Ida. Paris has to decide which goddess is the most beautiful, Hera, Athena, or Aphrodite. He has a golden apple to award, only one. And so the young man chooses—with the utter and self-evident arrogance of men. At the birth of Western culture, and mythologically speaking, before its biggest and most pervasive invention, namely war, Paris exercises choice. In this case it is between marriage and religion, embodied in the Goddess Hera; science and politics, embodied in Athena, Guardian of Athens; and beauty and desire, made manifest in Aphrodite. Paris arrives at a judgment that unleashes loss, discord, hate, and resentment, plunging Trojans and Greeks into the most male of occupations—war.
>
> The most important thing I want to say about your poetry, Ernesto, is that you did not follow Paris in arrogating choice to yourself. In your own way you have refuted that mythic story and overcome its destructive aspect, namely, the dividing, choosing, deciding that the old myth elaborates. You have not taken part in that exclusion that is always an insult to other forces of life. You did not place religion, politics, and love into a competitive struggle, in which a sovereign youngster chooses, decides. You kept them together. You resisted this ancient choice, this rift that runs through the world, and you have not fulfilled this mythic pattern.
>
> Your love poems are political, your psalms erotic, and your poems from Latin America's history repudiate coerced choice ever anew; it is as if the jungle had long choked off the wretched decisions of Troy. Your affirmation, your celebration of life is

encompassing, just as the threat to, and the experienced destruction of, life is one. It is the same enemy who interferes with our kissing and who furthers an elitist science, disconnected from life. It is the same severer who sterilizes living religion into formula and ritual, where no psalm may be recited in a new form lest it perhaps turn into a genuine prayer.

A PRAYER FOR NICARAGUA

Spread a large blanket
over the little country of volcanoes
so that the bomb-carrying planes may not find it
and the arson-murderers do not enter
and the president of the united dead
will forget the little country

Spread a large blanket
over the little country just four years old
so that the children may attend school
and also the older women like me
that coffee gets harvested and medicine distributed
and no one is forgotten

Spread a large blanket
held by all who love this country
the Virgin Mary has a coat
and Saint Francis a festive garment
that he threw at his rich father's feet
and Ho Chi Minh wore a peasant's shirt like Sandino
of all that fabric the blanket is woven

Spread a large blanket
of wishes breathing so much affection
that they become prayers
and love is the active word
that belongs to God
so the blanket comes from God
A dark blanket
spread to protect the hope of the poor
until the night ends
until finally the night ends

THE DISAPPEARED

In September 1979 I met an Argentinian minister in Buenos Aires who had been a student of mine in New York. He introduced his sister to me. Her husband had been interrogated by the police one Friday night in their home. Monday morning he prepared to go to work. He said that he had done nothing wrong or subversive; everybody should do his or her duty. And he was a Peronist. So their daughter left for school, their son for work, the mother for the office, and the father also left the house. That was in 1977. They have never seen him again; there is no trace, no clue.

This woman is one of thousands of people who have made application for *habeas corpus* actions. She is a relative of a disappeared, one of the mothers of the Plaza de Mayo, who every Thursday afternoon would gather in silent protest outside the house of government in the capital, until they were forbidden to do so. Government officials referred to them as *las locas*, the crazy ones, who refused to be silenced and who would go into hiding or leave the country only under the duress of threats. She was one of those who asked the simplest and most human of questions, one that is still being asked in all of Latin America: *¿Dónde están?* (Where are they?)

According to conservative estimates, at least 17,000 political prisoners were held in Latin American jails and camps at that time, that is, 1979–1980. Many people were driven into exile. At least 30,000 people had disappeared by then. The majority were probably murdered. I had very many conversations at that time in Chile and Argentina, and I recall them now, because to forget is a kind of dying. Military dictatorship has come to an end there in the meantime. This is a sign of hope, politically speaking; perhaps all this toil for human rights and solidarity was not altogether in vain.

In September 1979, I took part in a hearing on the disappeared held in Washington by a subcommittee of the Foreign Affairs Committee of the House of Representatives. "To disappear" (as an active verb) had taken on a new meaning, I learned there; it meant the involuntary disappearance of individuals through the complicity, permission, or conspiracy of government agencies in Argentina, Chile, Uruguay, and El Salvador, as well as other Latin American countries. To make someone disappear was and is a relatively new feature in the history of state terrorism; it is an international crime. It cannot be equated with the usual abduction, because no demand for ransom or other conditions that have to be met are associated with it. A person is apprehended, carried off, and subsequently held in solitary confinement. The fact that the various national secret services cooperated with the death squadrons is well-documented; bodies of people who had disappeared in Argentina showed up, for example, in Uruguay.

I came to know "disappearing" as a new crime, but there was no word yet for the criminals who "disappeared" people. Call them abductors, rapists, torturers, or murderers, but the crime of causing someone to disappear is not named thereby. For example, women in Chile looking for their spouses were told in tones of self-complacency: "Your marriage was in trouble, wasn't it? It's not that easy to get a divorce. . . . Why don't you think about whether the answer lies there?" It is part of these criminals' strategy to admit to nothing, to treat every case as a simple matter of "missing," and to refer one to another bureaucratic agency.

Victims generally referred to the criminals as "they": "they came to get him." The subject of the crime is the anonymous power whose name may be police or armed forces and who wears a uniform or street clothes; it no longer matters. State terrorism is difficult to lay hold of through the legal system.

Who are the victims of this crime? They come from every level of society: professors and students, labor leaders and union members. Some of them had never had political or ideological association. Others were connected in one way or another with people who had already disappeared.

Whether they be political activists, dissidents, unionists, or ordinary citizens who still feel for humanity or do not wish simply to observe the disappearance of their neighbors, the state declares them to be enemies of the state. All who think and feel for themselves are subversive. Reading works by Karl Marx or Sigmund Freud is dangerous, and to have a photocopier in the house is tantamount to hoarding explosives.

The harsh terror of concealing everything from the relatives of the disappeared is growing. Disappearing is itself a psychological torture for the relatives. They cannot verify whether the disappeared one is dead and, thus, must postpone their mourning again and again. They know that their relative is being tortured, they hear the horrible details, like eyes being torn out, but do not know what the one they love really has to endure. Hope and uncertainty thus combined become an instrument of torture.

A friend's mother told me that a group in North America asked her to visit prisoners in Villa Devoto. She was ready to go, but her daughter pressured her not to, "You have seven grandchildren in this country." "I did not go," she said hesitatingly. "Was that wrong?" A story of someone being broken.

Relatives were threatened, "Don't do anything if you want to see your husband again!" Even the disappeared were subjected to this terror of silence; some called home and said, "Please, no inquiries, I am fine, under the circumstances. Don't talk to anyone." What is one to do in such a situation? Very few of the "reappeared" are prepared to tell in which camps they had been held, preferring to remain silent about the torture they endured.

The simplest questions cannot be raised often enough: What does all this have to do with us? Is it true that human rights are indivisible? In what way is failure to help a human rights violation? Is maximizing profit a human rights violation when others do the dirty work of that enterprise? It is the goal of Amnesty International so to proscribe torture that it becomes "as unthinkable as slavery." The problem is the modern-day "slavery" that requires this torture. Slavery, total dependency, is the goal of the silent war of the rich against the poor we are involved in now. Torture is only one of the methods used to break the resistance against economic subjugation.

A broadsheet from the Chilean underground wrote the following to "those who are close to giving up and whose engagement is waning":

> This is where our greatest danger lies at the moment, which is also a great danger for our children and the coming generations: in the loss of moral sensitivity, the deliberate or at least accepted confusion between good and evil. There are things, after all, that we must cry out at least within our souls, if we may not say them out loud in the street. Otherwise, we will forget them. These lines were written so that you may not forget these things but wake up and burn bright like a torch.

But who in the First World of perpetrators hears such words? It seems cynical, in my view, to categorize them as "moralistic" and then to ignore them; such an attitude destroys its holders who let "their souls be exchanged," as the broadsheet claims. We can learn more from the resistance of oppressed peoples who, with old-fashioned ("moral") language, speak also for us and help us in organizing resistance. This is what I discern in that broadsheet:

> Awake, Chile, do not permit your soul to be exchanged. Your freedom-loving spirit used to sing different songs. Someday, will it again sing songs of freedom and justice? Watch how your children are being educated! Know what they are taught! Otherwise it may come to this—that while you sleep, they are told that it is good to kill one's brother, it is good to believe what the official press says, that truth is falsehood, and falsehood is truth.

And then I heard a wonderful story from Chile, a report of a miracle, a sign of hope that cannot be extinguished by the threat of torture, the terror of silence, and even the soft terror of our forgetfulness. A Presbyterian minister from the South of Chile distributed groceries that North American friends had sent to him. He was arrested and taken to Los Almas prison in Santiago. There, in a house the size of a small library, lived 150 men. He acted as chaplain to the other inmates and conducted daily Bible study and brief worship. Most of the men were socialists. He told me that he had never had such a congregation. When he was released, his fellow inmates wrote their names with burned-out matches on his back. It was November and warm outside; he was worried about perspiring. He was not searched before leaving and went straight to the Peace Committee. Most of the names of those men, who were thought to have disappeared, were still legible.

The names surfaced, written on the back of a prisoner. The hour of silence was at an end.

MOVEMENT FOR PEACE

I experienced December 12, 1979, as one of the bleakest days in Germany's postwar history. It was the day NATO reached its two-track decision on modernization of theater nuclear weapons in Europe. On that day I made a personal commitment to give the rest of my life to peace, part of which is justice for developing countries. It became clear to me then that the cry "Never again war!" is central in my life and deeply rooted in the story of my youth.

I did this not only for my children or for humankind as such, but also for myself. I was no longer able to laugh in a land of bombs. It not only harbored bombs to destroy—indeed, "overkill" our "enemies"—it also destroyed the people who paid for, produced, installed, and propagated them. The time after NATO's two-track decision was often compared to 1914. International tensions had reached such a level that as little as a minor stupidity by one of the leaders, or a small computer error, was enough to trigger the world catastrophe.

The word "peace," without qualifiers, appeared more and more rarely in the speeches of leading politicians. One did not wish to leave peace "quite so unprotected"; it had to be combined with "security." If one spoke loud enough and with the right amount of military logic about "security," the addition of "and peace" was no longer threatening. First things first: absolute security first. That concept became more and more neurotic.

A broadsheet of the U.S. peace movement declared that "the bombs are falling now." I came to learn much from this. I had thought that armament preparation was a matter of making arrangements for something that might come later, perhaps, or even not at all. But this preparation devoured our money, taxes, intelligence, and energy; it destroyed our own country and did not permit developing countries to attain peace or justice, or even to provide enough food to feed their people.

Getting involved meant organizing resistance. What we would need in the coming years—and what we were able to accomplish—was a broad, comprehensive resistance movement against militarism. It needed to embrace the political spectrum from the center to the left. It had to be a movement that stood up for peace, ready to get involved in taking the side of life. It had to do so nonviolently and, if no other option was left, illegally. I was sent a broadsheet from the resistance in Chile; to distribute it there was to risk one's very life. I became convinced that much of what was said in the context of that country could be appropriated for ours: "Involve yourself! Refuse to cooperate with death! Choose life! Do not permit your soul to be exchanged!"

Resistance found language and organization in many places. The Dutch Parliament refused to let medium-range missiles be stationed in the Netherlands; that was a bit of a rainbow in the sky. The Dutch, and particularly the Christians of the Reformed Church, gave perhaps the clearest and most unmistakable leadership to the resistance in Europe. Many Europeans were infected by this "Dutch disease."

The German peace movement, which came out into the open very clearly for the first time at the Protestant *Kirchentag* in Hamburg in 1981, knew itself to be rooted in the Judeo-Christian tradition. By "very clearly" I mean that it was as militant, nonviolent, and unlawful as Jesus and his followers were. Particularly women in Germany saw no reason whatsoever to regard themselves any longer as objects of male military politics. They coined the slogan: "If you don't resist, life is missed!" The engagement for peace grew in the women's movement. In the United States, women surrounded the Pentagon, holding hands; they were thrown into jail, only to return later in even larger groups.

I recalled at that time several experiences of the older peace movement of the '50s. Often, we were miserably small groups, among whom were many elderly women in worn-out overcoats. When I think back to those gatherings, I think of rain and cold, for I had only thin shoes and a light coat. And there was the deep feeling of being alone, in the figurative sense, of not being together, of being powerless, impotent. I missed the students, who were my own age and whose company I would have preferred.

Once, Martin Niemöller spoke to us. We perched on the tiny school desks of a primary school in Cologne-Ehrenfeld. I had tried to arouse a dashing young journalist's interest in what our group was about. His reply was, "A bunch of peace-ladies isn't worth the trouble." I have never forgotten that insult against peace, against older people who had, after all, experienced two world wars, and against women, who by definition are already not taken seriously.

For me they were women of an utterly unsentimental strength, who put their hands to everyday dirty work without much ado. Some had been conscripted to work in a munitions factory and were the first to note that their young women co-workers from the Ukraine were starving to death. So they shared with them the little they had themselves.

Radical forms of civil disobedience and resistance emerged from within the Catholic left in the United States. There were the Berrigan brothers, Daniel and Philip. From the time of the Vietnam War, they worked with many groups against arms production, which they referred to as "stealing from the poor." They are radical pacifists. For a long time, many people in Germany regarded the nonviolent resistance fighter Daniel Berrigan as a "nut" who, in the best old tradition of pacifism, merely "gave testimony" without any political consideration. In the '80s it became increasingly clear to me how such resistance fighters actually represented the salt within the whole peace movement. Their readiness, their freedom, and their preparedness, if need be, to give their lives in opposition to Moloch, the Big Beast from the abyss, slowly radicalized more and more Christians. Among them were bishops and church leaders such as Raymond Hunthausen, archbishop of Seattle, who refused to pay taxes.

This Catholic resistance movement was a historical novelty in the U.S.; even during the Vietnam War, the Catholic church was slow and quite late in offering resistance against the genocide in Indochina. In the days of the peace movement, however, it was a leader and went far beyond the moderate campaign, for example, in support of Freeze, the program to halt the construction, testing, and stationing of nuclear weapons.

In 1981, friends of mine, among them the Berrigans, were tried in a court in Norristown, Pennsylvania. They had named their group The Plowshares 8, after the words of the prophet Isaiah: "They shall beat their swords into plowshares" (Isa. 2:4). The eight men and women, among them a Catholic nun and a mother of six children, had entered the General Electric plant in King of Prussia, Pennsylvania, where nuclear weapons were being produced. They damaged two nuclear warheads and spilled human blood on secret blueprints. Apprehended by military police, they were handed over to the local police and arrested. They were charged with breaking and entering, criminal conspiracy, trespassing, insurrection, causing a disturbance (by which the prosecution presumably meant to identify the spiritual hymns of peace the accused had been singing), theft, and provoking arrest. Daniel Berrigan was sentenced to ten years in prison; his brother, Philip, to three years. In critiquing the United States' arms production, Philip Berrigan said, "We must take greater risks than we ever did before."

Forms of civil disobedience also emerged in Germany; hundreds of thousands took to the streets in impressive demonstrations of protest. One journalist, reporting on the 300,000 demonstrators who had gathered in Bonn on October 10, 1981, noted the size but badly missed the import of the gathering and could find nothing more imaginative to say than: "Just as in the days of Hitler." Such blindness and distortion of reality outraged me more than anything had for a long time. It is part of conservative ideology that people's reasons for organizing and taking to the streets are not important, but truly it is the phenomenon of critical mass itself that is threatening and dangerous. It made no difference that, since 1980, millions of Europeans expressed their desire for peace in completely nonviolent demonstrations; friends of peace were again and again depicted as being violent, or ready to use violence. The actual course of events was the very opposite; we saw more and more clearly that submissions, letters to members of parliament, and handbills alone were futile against the arrogance of power that expressed itself most blatantly in militarism.

Slowly many friends of peace moved toward methods of nonviolent actions that were contrary to the law. We decided to announce blockades, which are unlawful, and to blockade places like Mutlangen, where nuclear missiles were stationed, and Waldfischbach with its poison gas. Being arrested, criminalized, tried, and sentenced were important events in my life. They not only produced publicity but also bonded together all blockaders, young and old, prominent and unknown.

The other side within the church campaigned under the slogan Secure Peace and supported arms production. Prominent theologians like Wolfhart Pannenberg, Trutz Rendtorff, Gerhard Ebeling, and others, laypeople and scholars, on the basis of their Christian sense of responsibility, considered unilateral disarmament to be a mistake and endangering the peace. They were of the opinion that, given the current level of military technology, which is to say nuclear war, West Germany could be successfully defended. The supporters of the initiative "Living without Armament" denied that view. The question of peace showed plainly how people today understand Christianity, how it drove them to take a stand and make a confession of their faith, led them into a *status confessionis*. Taking a stand on one's confession of Christ has always played a clarifying role in the history of the church. The differentiation that arose around the question of peace was of much more importance than that resulting from traditional denominational differences.

I once stood with a group of students in front of the German Armed Forces officers' academy in Hamburg; we sang and prayed in the cold and snow. We spoke of our personal fears and hopes. Standing by the huge fence that surrounded the area, one young man told us that four years ago, when he was on the other side of the fence, he thought we were crazy. But now, he was glad that he was on this side and that he knew why. The onetime officer was now a theology student. In that situation, I had a glimpse of the oneness of struggle and contemplation. There we stood, having read a prophetic text from the Bible, freezing and feeling helpless. But it would have occurred to none of us to pick up rocks. We knew again how difficult the struggle is and how long, how unendingly long it could last.

I had a conversation with Dan Berrigan about the experience of powerlessness and despair. He said this to me: "There are situations when you can't ask about success, because that question will get you down. If you make succeeding your primary concern, you have already capitulated to the system. Of course, there is an experience of powerlessness, but it must not paralyze you. Civil courage has to do with self-respect, with the self-assertion of human dignity. And it comes before success."

I thought then about my mother predicting that I would know what it was to be unsuccessful. I also felt a kind of Protestant defiance, something of what Martin Luther expresses in his famous hymn: "And were the world all devils o'er and ready to devour us, we do not fear them all so sore, from God they cannot hold us." I recall a peace worship in a church filled to overflowing that ended with this hymn, "A Mighty Fortress Is Our God." I had the feeling that I had never really understood that hymn; all those old-fashioned images of devils seeking to devour us, of the prince of this world looking so grim. Suddenly it seemed to fit, because it was related to a life situation.

In the movement for peace, my faith was fully alert to a resurrection from death, the death in which we then found ourselves. I was also fully awake to the fact that there could still be a meaningful struggle for peace after the defeats, that is, after the missiles had been stationed. The stationing had been a defeat, not only of peace but also of democracy and self-determination, a defeat of everything the West stood for.

Once, when I was particularly depressed, a friend and pacifist from Holland told me something very beautiful: "The people who worked to build the cathedrals in the Middle Ages never saw them completed. It took

two hundred years and more to build them. Some stone-cutter some-where sculpted a beautiful rose; it was his life's work, and it was all he ever saw. But he never entered into the completed cathedral. But one day, the cathedral was really there. You must imagine peace the same way."
Those words helped me a lot. It was good to know: I was participating in building a cathedral, and I knew that someday it would be completed. Just as slavery was abolished, so war also will be abolished, though beyond my lifetime.

Since then, I find that we can truly love only when we are so anchored in life that we are connected with the people who lived before us and with those yet to be born. When we destroy that connection and limit ourselves singly to our existence, we destroy ourselves. I found it important to take to the streets for the dead of Hiroshima and Nagasaki. They went with us, and those who held power in their hands knew it and sensed that we had an invisible army with us. We were not alone; we were far more numerous than the arms-buildup protagonists, because they always have against them the dead, whom war has cheated out of their lives.

AGAINST APARTHEID

About thirty years ago, I had an experience that made plain how very old is the fight against the rule of violence and its accomplices. On a visit to friends in East Berlin, I brought along a last-minute purchase, a big bag of oranges. Everyone was glad to finally see oranges again, that is, everyone except Elisabeth. At that time, my friend Elisabeth Adler was directing the Protestant lay academy in East Berlin. She looked at the oranges and exclaimed, "From South Africa? I don't eat such things." I have never been so mortified as I was at that moment; since then, I do not buy fruit without first checking where it is from. I learned something about the pride and the outrage of a Christian woman from East Germany, as well as about the apartheid that lived in me.

There are two kinds of compassion, childish and genuine. One is to regret the terrible things that happen in so many places of the world: we feel affected and shaken and are ready to give money; we think of the victims, but then put the situation behind us. Our day-to-day life is not touched; we go on living as before with apartheid in our heads and our hearts, separating us from "those poor South African blacks."

Like every strong, immediate feeling, compassion can go in one of two directions. It can set itself apart from analysis, comprehension, and informed knowledge and remain childish, so to speak, and for that reason be quickly forgotten. Or it can become probing, persistent, and self-critical in its questioning, and it can train itself in analysis. Our media, to a large extent, opted for childish compassion and ruled out genuine compassion, the one that goes to the roots.

Once people are sensitized, they come to know fairly accurately where it is that they can alter their behavior. Anyone who is reasonably alert has numerable chances to withhold participation and to say No to certain consumer goods, for example, or to an excessive consumption of energy or meat and, instead, raise critical questions about what industry produces. And there are also chances to change one's lifestyle and one's political consciousness, to join an organization seeking to achieve certain goals.

A number of years ago in the United States, I met two young white students from South Africa. We talked a bit; I asked them about the situation in their country, the blacks there, and in particular about Soweto. I asked whether they had been there, whether people had running water in their shacks or barracks, electricity or oil—all very specific questions. They had no idea; they knew the golf courses and tennis courts where they played, the small schools they attended. They talked as if they were travel agents. They told me how beautiful their country was, but they had no answers to my questions. They simply did not know. They knew nothing of the reality of their own country. What was apparent was an invisible barrier no less horrible than the Berlin Wall.

Most people in my country also lived behind such a wall, because apartheid was not merely a South African problem: it is a problem of the rich and so-called First World. Yes, we knew the tasty, inexpensive bananas and the good coffee, but our orientation remained one of tourists, and not one of sisters or brothers.

The General Secretary of the South African Council of Churches, Christiaan Beyers Naudé, once asked me on what or in whom I grounded my hope for change. I told him that, above all, I placed my hope in women who despair so deeply in the culture we live in—the cultural apartheid and the brutality and false spirit of competition—that they have to pull away from it simply to remain or even to become human. Being Christian, I continued, will become increasingly difficult and costly in the next twenty years.

For me, a beautiful example of conversion was the protest movement of Protestant women who organized and then implemented a boycott of South African fruit. When they began this action in the early '80s, they were laughed at. The Protestant church of Germany blocked their money and declared that a man would have to administer it for them since they were obviously incompetent themselves. Earlier in my life, I too had believed that women's work was involved primarily in darning socks; I had no idea what astonishing things these women were doing. During the boycott, they went to the wholesalers and the markets—at five in the morning!—and said to those preparing to sell their merchansdise: "These oranges from South Africa taste of blood. Don't sell them anymore. Don't participate in this slavery."

It is a peculiar, indispensable experience that everyone can have who refuses to be silenced and lacking in judgment—that the weak (through unified struggle and the like) become strong. Those who are being killed create life. That was precisely what those Protestant women taught us. They also were scorned and humiliated. With tears in her eyes, a young woman once told me how when they spoke at a supermarket, people listened to her male co-worker but dismissed her with the comment, "What do you know about that, anyway?" Swallowing defiantly, she added, "But I'll go back!" And so, the women stayed put, living little stories of the strength of the weak, the power of the powerless—little stories of the resurrection from the death wherein we have taken up residence.

For over two decades, South Africa challenged me to express my compassion a bit more seriously. This compassion became active, self-critical; it entered into my everyday life, my meals, my money transactions, my relationship to others. I could not have the murdered school children of Soweto in my head and then forget them in my "ordinary" life. They called on me—and many other women—to act: Close your bank accounts! On Monday morning, go to the branch managers of those who aid in the torture, the resettlement, the killing! Do not say: I'm too young, I'm unemployed, I don't have a bank account. This active compassion declares: South Africa is burning, and they pour more oil on the fire. They throw eight-year-olds into jail, and you pay for it! Have we not had enough racism in this country? And enough followers and accomplices, enough people who block out everything with the refrain, "But we didn't know"? Tell the people inside and outside the banks what is going on and why that police state has not yet collapsed; tell them who and what maintains this disdain of human beings, and also who profits from it, and why more and more innocent people will die.

The banks in Germany delayed the long-apparent economic collapse of the apartheid regime. Their politics of support for the white minority was blind to the history that lies behind us; they had learned nothing from it. Nor did such politics see what lies before us, what may be delayed but not stopped. Delay helped no one. And often, so often, the hope for a reform of apartheid proved to be an illusion and a betrayal of black people's living hopes. Every form of opposition was to be suffocated. All whose ideas were not those of the government were stripped of their rights and banned without explanation. And, at the same time, the solidarity of the many friends of justice throughout the world was to be prohibited and destroyed. It was as if we were being told, "You shall not love your neighbor."

Belatedly, Fulbert and I closed our account with the Dresdner Bank in April 1985. Credits received from that bank financed the expanding militarization of South Africa. Dresdner Bank held shares in the guilt of apartheid that every day created bloody victims among the black population. Shortly before, Citibank in New York had pulled out of the dirty business. We demanded that Dresdner Bank also terminate its business relations to South Africa and not simply ignore respect for human rights when it comes to banking.

We were invited to a conversation. There, representatives of the bank emphasized that, like us, they were opposed to apartheid, but for them an economic boycott was an improper and unacceptable change agent. It so happened that on the same day, there was a demonstration in Hamburg against the system of what Jesse Jackson called "The Fourth Reich." During our discussion in the beautiful old house on the Jungfernstieg, the sound of thousands of voices ascended from the street, crying, "*Deutsche Waffen, deutsches Geld morden weiter in der Welt.*" ("German weapons, German money, go on killing in the world.")

The women and their boycott were not deterred by those who argued that it was of no use. After ten years of patient and persevering toil, they got at least two big supermarket chains to stop selling apartheid fruit. "At the urgent request of our customers, we no longer import South African fruit," they announced. This victory prompted the women to multiply their efforts a hundredfold.

And so I plead for compassion that is wide awake and strong: Justice is a sun that ought to shine, in your small corner and mine, and on our friends. And finally, it needs to shine into the darkest corners of the executive suites. It took a long time for the sun to reach them, but nothing and no one—neither money, nor military or secret police—could block this sun. It shone—God blessed Africa.

When apartheid came to an end, I wished that the Protestant church in Germany had rung all church bells and expressed thanks to the women who had organized the boycott movement. Of course, nothing of the kind was done. But I had another good experience. A woman whom I did not know telephoned and asked for a poem that had been read at a celebration in the spring of 1994. I had watched the free election in South Africa with enthusiasm, forgetting about my old poem from the early '80s. It is a rare happiness when a vision comes to fulfillment and poetry about liberation is more than dreams:

NKOSI SIKELEL' I AFRIKA

Everytime I hear the hymn of liberation
I think of the school children
who one day will sing—
in their own language—
God protect Africa
And sometimes I think—don't laugh at me—
it will be in my own lifetime
I shall be able to sing along
not only from the heavens
but with all Seraphim and Cherubim here
In Hamburg-Altona I shall sing
perhaps my voice will be very thin
but sing with you I shall
Three days long we shall hold the feast
and Robben Island shall be an island
Soweto a young city
And God shall protect Africa
and I shall sing
one way or another

NEXT YEAR IN JERUSALEM

In the spring of 1980, my friend Robert McAfee Brown took me along on a visit to Elie Wiesel, the Jewish writer. Himself a survivor of Auschwitz, Wiesel had introduced the word "holocaust," so that neither would Hitler's language be kept alive in terms such as "final solution" or "extermination," nor neutrality flourish in words like "catastrophe" or "genocide."

At first, the conversation in Wiesel's apartment near Central Park in New York focused on planning for the Holocaust Monument. Elie Wiesel chaired the commission whose major difficulty seemed to be to determine how victims were to be identified and included. Was it to be Jews only, who had been destroyed like vermin? Was it not also Gypsies? And homosexuals? More and more ethnic groups came forward, asking that their dead be remembered: Estonians, Lithuanians, Latvians, Kurds, and more. As we spoke, the telephone rang repeatedly; at every ring, Wiesel flinched. A diminutive, agitable human being, he kept lifting the receiver himself, because, indeed, the matter was so acute: Weighing the dead against the dead, claims of suffering against claims of suffering was something gruesome, impossible, and unavoidable.

Eventually, our conversation turned to more personal matters. Wiesel told us something about his relationship with his then eight-year-old son. Every evening, father and son spent an hour together that had been firmly fixed. Wiesel said that was the reason he did not like to travel, or wherever possible, took his son along. Certain rules governed the time together: Both could ask whatever they wished; both were to answer as best they could. For example, the boy would ask his father to talk about his school years. "What was it like when you were a boy?" Or, "Is the teacher still alive? What happened then? Is the cherry tree still in Uncle's garden?" And the father did not answer. He did not speak. He was silent. One day the boy asked a strange question. "Was that before or was it after?" The father had told the boy nothing about the deportations, the extermination camps, the gas. But the boy knew something had happened and depicted it in the words "before" and "after." "It was before, wasn't it, Father?" he said. At one time or another, the father must have told him what had happened between before and after.

When I heard a live performance of Bach's St. Matthew's Passion for the first time again after the war, in 1946, the mighty chorale, "His blood be upon us and our children," had been deleted. What had gone "before" had become impossible "after." The event had soiled the words; thought and image had altered their meaning.

Nothing tells me of my own aging as plainly as the very impossibility of communicating to my descendants what Auschwitz means for my generation. Of course, I try to do so and, of course, I find it quite monstrous when people who understand quantum theory do not know words like "selection," "ramp," "Cyclon B." Of course, I have asked again and again how we could transmit our history of infamy, yet I feel the generation gap and how different the generations are. How can one hand down the feelings of shame and guilt so that they will not be forgotten? How can a national identity come into being that will not "work through" our past but pass it on?

True, I fight against my own aging, against my experience of becoming a throwaway commodity. But I also fight against anyone in my country who proclaims that "we are once again somebodies," a sentiment in which a renunciation of the feeling of collective shame is discernible.

Auschwitz did not end in Auschwitz. "What can we do?" I asked Elie Wiesel. Jewish tradition teaches that we are to pray and do justice. Nobody is to come along and allege not to have known. To do justice and to pray means refusing to let oneself be used for each and every purpose; it means offering resistance, giving bread to the hungry instead of to makers of ever more sophisticated weapons. To pray means not to despair. To pray is to contradict death. Praying means collecting oneself, reflecting, gaining clarity about where our lives are really moving and what we want to do with them. It means to remember and therein come to resemble the God who remembers. It means harboring wishes for ourselves and our children; uttering them aloud and quietly, together with others and alone, and therein coming to resemble more and more the human beings we were meant to be.

When I met Elie Wiesel a second time, in April 1982, once again in his apartment, I wanted to speak with him about the subject of "Heimat"— "home." I asked him whether there was a place anywhere in the world where he felt at home. I was asking this question of someone who had survived Auschwitz, but I also put it to myself, hoping to receive from the conversation not so much answers as a better insight into the question of "being at home."

Elie Wiesel delineated three approaches to the subject, three basic aspects of possibly being at home. The first is that we should look for *Heimat* in time rather than space. The second is that to go back to one's own childhood is a manner of returning home. The third is that, for him, Jerusalem is home.

In our conversation, these three basic aspects were interwoven; they pervaded one another. "I feel at home in my city, in Jerusalem," was his spontaneous reply to my initial question. But right away he connected it with the recollection of his childhood in Eastern Europe. Wiesel felt at home in the time of his childhood in Romania; the time before the destruction of everything that could mean *Heimat* to an Eastern European Jew. In the words "Jerusalem," "my city," "Yes, Jerusalem," the first thing I discerned was a distancing from his present life in New York. When someone asks me about *Heimat*, I feel that way, too. I also want to say: Not here; not now. No place, nowhere.

Heimat has so much to do with childhood, rootedness, and origin that every attempt of an exiled person to name it in another language must fail. Wiesel and I spoke English to each other; he remarked that later he had learned French and wrote his books in that language. He understood the German word "*Heimat*," which I had not wanted to translate. But none of our languages is the Romanian of his childhood. And so the language we use makes us conscious of a sense of being a bit homeless, without *Heimat*.

As the noises of 84th Street rose up, it became clear to me why New York draws foreigners so powerfully: This city makes not even the tiniest false promise that *Heimat* is what it offers. The numerous, diverse neighborhoods of this city with their names, languages, artisans, customs, foods, smells—they tell of an earlier *Heimat* that once was. Not here, they say. Once upon a time, yes, but not now. It made me realize how much we need both to be at home and to remain a stranger. For me, Manhattan is at once a symbol of *Heimat* and homelessness.

"I feel at home in my city, in Jerusalem. In that place, I have the feeling of having been there for many, many years. I love Jerusalem. It's true that I live in New York. Do I feel the need to be away from Jerusalem? There is in our tradition the legend of the heavenly Jerusalem for which we are always on the lookout. This longing cannot be destroyed. We need to get there."

I thought of the Passover liturgy and the words, "Next year in Jerusalem." "Does that refer to the heavenly or the earthly Jerusalem?" I asked.

"Both, really. Both. Jerusalem is as spiritual as it is physical. But not only the place; the time, too. For surely that is the meaning of the Passover liturgy. This year we are slaves, next year we shall be free. There is always a projection into the future that is also a projection into the human dimension, a vision of humanity directed into the sphere of the human. Today, that sounds ironic. But that is mostly what it meant. Jerusalem—humanize the future more and more."

We spoke of Jerusalem as an intersection of the dimensions of being at home. Here the recollections of his little town in Transylvania were most alive for Wiesel. Nowhere else in the world does he remember his childhood as clearly and vividly. In Jerusalem, he digs a pebble from the ground on his walks and puts it in his pocket, just as he did as a child.

Heimat is a place where memories may stay and are not sent away. It is a place of harmony or—Wiesel corrected himself as he talked—a place where dissonances turn into harmony. He spoke of the security a child has because it knows that black is black, good is good, evil is evil. Even in Auschwitz, children lived out of such security. The feelings came much later. Earlier this certainty was present, offering a kind of protection and resistance, "an astonishing quality of resistance."

But who creates *Heimat*? I wanted to know. "Often, it is the children; my boy does for me. I believe that the children do much more for us than we for them." In the end, we spoke of Cain and Abel. I asked whether we would not rather be Abel than Cain, if we had the choice. Wiesel repudiated my pacific dream and stressed that both brothers were accountable for the other's destiny. I wanted to know in what sense Abel was responsible. "He was silent when Cain needed him. Abel said nothing."

We could not avoid speaking again and again of preparations for war and of the peace movement. The expression "nuclear holocaust" came to be used more and more at that time. Did we have the right to talk that way? Elie Wiesel is one of those survivors who helped in getting the word "holocaust" used today specifically for the mass murder of European Jewry, so that the fiery holocaust of six million has absorbed every other form of holocaust-burnt offering. Were we right, I wanted to know, when we applied that word to those who planned the limited and winnable atomic war? Contrary to other Jewish spokespeople, Wiesel immediately gave me a positive response. Not only can we speak that way, he said, we must.

On September 30, 1988, the Nobel Peace laureate turned 60. I had been invited to attend a conference in his honor in St. Louis, Missouri. Once again I experienced something that in Germany is no longer possible: I encountered the spirit of Judaism. Not that there are no conferences now and then where we might meet individual Jewish artists; what we miss—and more painfully so when one surmises what it must have meant—is the ambiance, the climate, the world of Jewish life. Never before had I dined—kosher, of course—accompanied with Hebrew blessings and festive speeches, full of chutzpah and humor. And all that together with about a thousand Jewish people, many of whom were children of survivors or relatives of the murdered, gathered here for the occasion in the foyer of a large hotel. Elie Wiesel was honored with the "tree of life," which meant that a forest will be planted in Israel in his honor.

What about this spirit of Judaism after its greatest catastrophe, the destruction of European Jews? The conference was not only a meeting with an Auschwitz survivor but with a whole group of artists, historians, physicians, philosophers, and theologians. They had gathered to talk together about Elie Wiesel's first book, *Night*, which had been published thirty-five years before. It appeared first in Argentina, written in Yiddish, and was titled *Und di Welt hot geschwign* (*And the World Kept Silent*); today the book is compulsory reading in many colleges and schools. When will it be so at home? I wondered.

Then I listened to an old, fragile psychiatrist from Oslo who had been in Auschwitz with Wiesel. Dr. Leo Etinger talked about what it had meant to be a physician there. Declaring a patient recovered and sending her or him back meant their return to hell. Not treating patients meant giving up on them. "You were my healer," Elie Wiesel said to him later, and he replied, "That is the best thing anyone can be told."

The subject of friendship as a search for understanding of one another occupied the whole day, as did that of not giving up. Wiesel said, "The essence of Jewishness is never to give up. Everything that has to do with Auschwitz leads in the long run into the dark. And what is the dark? The questions must remain questions; there are no final answers." One of his key phrases that is spoken again and again is "and yet, and yet"; it expresses this Jewish character of not giving up.

Wiesel had another, noteworthy encounter with a physician, a surgeon in a New York hospital. When Wiesel worked as a reporter with the United Nations, he was run over by a taxi and suffered more than forty fractures. An ambulance took him to the hospital; two hospitals did not want to admit the penniless foreigner who carried no insurance. Finally, Dr. Braunstein admitted him and worked on him for months. A friendship grew from this encounter.

Franklin Littell, a philospher of religion, is often referred to as the father of holocaust research in the United States; he subjected the scholarly treatment of this subject to the following, brilliant critique. "Sociologists speak of 'racial prejudice,' psychologists of mass psychology, political scientists of dictatorship, and still others of the consequences of brutality and sadism. But all of them are attempts at minimizing, which in their language functions no differently than the infamous Wannsee Conference of 1942, where the final solution of the Jewish Question was decided on."

Verharmlosung—to minimize something or to render it harmless— was one of the concepts that were used in German in this context. The German historians' debates on the uniqueness and historical meaning of the Holocaust appear utterly peculiar to someone who has spent a day together with survivors, rescuers, and bystanders. It takes on the features of an unconscious specialty of German culture.

I had been invited as a Christian theologian and tried to contribute something on the subject of shame and memory. Whoever does not remember, whoever pretends not to have known, and whoever did not want to know later on or blathers with Chancellor Helmut Kohl about "the grace of a late birth" has understood nothing at all. God is memory, and that is why to remember is to approach God. To forget, to repress, is a way of getting rid of God.

"To remember" has a fine double meaning. Literally, it means to become once again a member of the whole. Whoever does not *re*member is *dis*membered, excluded, without a place in the family of nations.

Elie Wiesel responded to our several contributions and thanked us in an easy manner pervaded by Jewish humor; it made bearable the official tone of the event and the all too lofty compliments and rituals. "It was because of the questions that I entered philosophy, and it was because of the answers that I left it again," he said to the philosophers. To William Heyen, the lyric poet, he said: "Why should I be a second-class lyric poet when in reality I am a first-class reader of poetry?" Facing me, he spoke movingly about the children of the Germans he had come to know. He criticized the notion of collective guilt without erasing that of collective shame. He referred to encounters with young Germans who had confided in him that they had learned only at age twenty of their fathers' complicity and now tried to live with that reality.

It was an unusual time with one of the great storytellers of our time, a witness to history and—as it seemed to me—a Hasidic rabbi who had grown ever more pious. In the course of the discussion, someone asked whether the Holocaust spelled the end of Judaism. The answer—not from Elie Wiesel but from a younger Jewish woman—was no, but the end of Christianity. That reply held me captive for the whole day and has never let me go. I must hear it and want to refute it, not by arguments but by a life before the One who has also told me what is good and what is required of me (Micah 6:8).

SANCTUARY

Among my most powerful recollections of the United States are the encounters with the movement to provide sanctuary to people fleeing repression and terror in Central America. In November 1985, I had some contacts with sanctuary in Arizona. This was very important for me. I hiked with Sr. Darleen Nigorski in the Arizona desert; we were accompanied by two nuns who were also Sisters of St. Francis. Our path, a modest upward climb, led to the Sabrina Valley, below a chain of mountains that constantly changed colors and cast different shadows. There were red fruit on the cacti; I tasted one.

We walked to the sisters' residence, Holy Cross, for a spaghetti dinner. Right away I felt at home: there was no superelegant bathroom, everything was simple, there was water and wine to drink, and the poor women of the neighborhood came and went. One of the old women looked like a German high school instructor; she told us about a conference on racism she had just attended. During the day, all were busy in soup kitchens or other work programs.

Darleen turned out to be someone who knew clearly what she wanted. When the priest with whom she had worked in the Guatemalan countryside was murdered, she had to leave. She became one of the leading figures in the sanctuary movement but, because she was a woman, had less public visibility and was less noticed.

Even though I was very tired, I accompanied Darleen to an evening worship service of the Catholic Worker. The liturgy was simple: a Scripture reading, weak singing accompanied by guitar. It was a colorful mix of people who had come to worship: a taciturn vagrant, a neurotic forty-year-old woman who absolutely wanted to drink all of the communion wine, a single mother and her six-year-old who made unspeakable noises with his nose, a very old woman, a student. Maria, one of the sisters, gave the meditation and played the guitar. The disturbances were taken in stride, and I pondered the meaning of "humility." I had to read the text about truth and Pontius Pilate from the Gospel of John; I felt my fatigue rest on me like lead, and I entered deeply into the prayer—for refugees and the homeless.

The next evening we drove to West Tucson. The whole city is surrounded by hills that develop the most incredible colors at night. I met for an evening of reflection with people on trial for activities in the sanctuary movement. How different those people were! There was Sr. Darleen, wholly marked by her experience in Guatemala and the war against the desolately poor that the Americans waged under the category of counter-insurgency and fighting terrorism. Then there was Jim Corbett, a Quaker and friend of nature, who knew every trail across the border into Mexico and was a stubborn individualist to boot. And John Five, a very congregation-minded Presbyterian minister who brought many refugees across the border and was now on trial. The others were mostly young people who "just because they were Christians," as they said, could not bear the thought that people who had done nothing wrong were sent back to torture and death.

I made a few remarks about a theology of resistance to come, at the end of the Constantinian age, trying to diminish the fear of those who were present for strongly or "pure" religious motives. We learn resistance, I said, as the religio-political task given to Christians of the First World. It was a very serious conversation we had in the multiangled house, serenaded by crickets under the light of the moon, with the saguaros of the desert standing guard. At midnight I was taken to the airport and later was glad to be back again in old, damp, raw, terrible, beloved New York.

A few days later I wrote my newly won friends this letter:

Dear Friends in the Sanctuary Movement:

I write to thank you for the days I was allowed to spend with you in Tucson. Thank you for taking me with you into the beauty of the desert and into the labyrinth of the American legal system. Above all, thank you for your patience with my many questions. Some of them are still sitting, like birds in my tree waiting to be fed.

I wrote letters to friends in Germany to make the sanctuary movement known over there. In our movements, international exposure is very important to keep the struggle alive, seeing as the enemy's organization is both international and multinational. The sanctuary movement has given me courage because it has shown new ways of standing with the victims of injustice. To make this known in Europe may strengthen Christian groups there. Right now, the rights of refugees are hotly debated in Switzerland, and in Hamburg a seafarer's family from the Philippines found asylum in a church. What I try to express in the word "internationalism" came to me in a strong feeling I had that night of our miniretreat: In Europe, we need people like you in the U.S.A.

I am worried still about the tensions between the group in Chicago and that in Tucson. I wonder what that means for us all who seek to develop forms of resistance against the systems of terror that we live in. What may we learn from these two camps in relation to the future of the *pueblo de Dios*? I am convinced that the difficulties you experience in the sanctuary movement are typical of most Christian groups that take up an engagement on behalf of the victims of state terrorism. Those tensions are unavoidable. I have been part of similar debates in the group around the Political Evensong we conducted in the late '60s in Cologne as well as in the peace movement since the early '80s.

I think that it is a dimension of our First World reality that so many engaged and wonderful human beings are afraid to be regarded as "political," and to be drawn into something unknown to them. I would suggest that you do not regard the differences between the sanctuary workers in Tucson, Chicago, and elsewhere as rigorously exclusive options on the basis of differing theological and ethical principles. I rather tend to see them as phases of consciousness-raising, wherein different points of view and plans of action have their own identity.

The direction of the process must be irreversible, however. This means quite simply that we all must grow more profoundly into love. This growth signifies a politization of conscience, in utter contrast to our customary Christian education: It is so very busy privatizing our spiritual strength, to anchor it in the family and the individual. This arrests spiritual strength on the level of charity as interpreted by the bourgeois within us. Love that does not venture beyond its own horizon, and does not dare to search mercilessly for the foundation of terror, is not love.

Why are people so scared of being put into a particular corner? They are afraid—and I also hear this from some of you—of being "co-opted" by an anonymous apparatus and its political "ideology." They would prefer decentralization to a central committee and pluralism to a specific party line and party rhetoric. They have engaged themselves locally in concrete work for refugees and are suspicious of a national organization. They want to help the refugees without becoming entangled in an "ideology," which is what they call every political analysis, rightist or leftist.

It seems to me that they most simply want to be disciples of Christ, followers in the practical sense of doing mercy, wherever they are needed. When the movement becomes "too political," they feel run over, or misused as religious people. I realized just how serious the debate was when I heard talk of refugees being "used" for political purposes. It seems to me the movement's integrity is at stake the moment one group in the movement makes the state's rhetoric its own and uses it against another group. That integrity rules out every form of manipulation of refugees as well as every attempt to conceal the causes of why the refugees are there at all.

When I reflected on the spiritual situation of the movement's uneasy grassroots workers, I thought about the Bible, especially the structure of the New Testament. When you compare the first three Gospels with the letters of Paul, you find a similar tension between the good news, the healing, feeding, the doing of God's work on the one hand, and the reflections and the praxis of the Apostle Paul on the other. In the New Testament as a whole, we sense the growing need for a more completely organized and theoretically coherent development that the early Christians must also have sensed.

Those of you who know me as a feminist may be surprised that I dare to say something in praise of Paul and his life's work. But being with you in Tucson helped me understand anew how much the early Jesus movement needed Paul. It needed an organizational structure for the growing movement and, increasingly, a "theory" about what love meant in its world. The movement needed all those pamphlets and broadsheets that Paul produced. (In certain circles they are called "Pastoral Epistles.") Communicators were needed between those tiny groups. The movement had to spell out what it meant by love, faith, being made in the image of God, freedom, and so forth. In other words, it needed "theory," also known as "theology."

There is a difference between Paul and his friends in Rome, Corinth, and Chicago, on the one hand, and the friends of Jesus in Galilee and Tucson, on the other. In my view, it consists of two factors: *theory* and *organization*. Both are necessary components that grow from the commitment to love our neighbors as ourselves. But both are marked by a certain coldness that makes it difficult for grassroots people to busy themselves with theory and organization.

I think that the early Christians had to make a conscious decision for both the theory and the organization of love. It was a conscious decision for a sociopolitical analysis that was present already in the teaching of Jesus. And it was a conscious step into the organization that at that time was called *ecclesia*, the church. It was no "ideological" decision, abstracted from and befogging reality, even though Paul's teaching was decried as ideology by the propagandists of Imperial Rome and its "peace." Instead, it was an analysis of the historical situation under the "principalities and powers" of Rome, an analysis that gave the early Christians clarity to understand, and courage to resist the system.

The situation of Christians at the end of the twentieth century has many similarities to early Christianity. The militarization of our globe—and beyond it—in the interest of an omnipotent, omniscient, and omnipresent system of state terrorism produces misery, oppression, torture, death squads, and, as a consequence, refugees. The sanctuary movement is a response of those who have heard the cries of the oppressed. With its basis in the depoliticized citizens of the U.S. middle class, it lays claim with great integrity to the best traditions of the history of North America. The movement is an attempt at long last to "lay hold of" those traditions of the law—from the emancipation of slaves to the civil rights movement and the fight for human rights internationally and nationally—by legal means and, if necessary, even by civil disobedience.

In the process of taking possession of one's own history, it becomes apparent how necessary it is within the structures of evil that there be a movement from spontaneous mercy to love. Love is that power that frees in others "that which is of God"; love reveals the hidden strength of "the knowledge of Yahweh" in others. To know Yahweh means to live justice. Love gives us the strength to do so; the conscious decision for doing analysis and being in favor of organizing is one of the deeds of love.

The deed is simpler for people who are directly threatened by state terrorism, namely, the refugees themselves. But when we listen to them, we have to understand their critique of every form of cheap charity that ignores the sources of oppression. As one of the principles of liberation theology states: The poor are our teachers. When we hear them, we are drawn into analyzing the production of refugees and learn to name those who sustain the real terrorism because they derive profit from it. "Evil has an address," Bertolt Brecht said in the '30s. "It has a telephone number." We still have to learn this lesson. We need to go beyond giving aid in catastrophes and beyond charitable action, and trust the Holy Spirit who is not afraid of organization, structure, and theory, but uses them all for her purposes.

God bless the sanctuary movement and grant all of us peace with justice.

Dorothee

Today, in the late '90s, I can see something of that blessing also in Germany. On account of the undermining of the right to refuge for the persecuted, a right enshrined in German Fundamental Law, asylum in churches has gained new actuality. This is a beautiful sign of the power of the biblical tradition. However problematic that tradition is in relation to questions such as that of human sexuality, it is clear in relation to the question of refugees, including those whom we disqualify as economic refugees. To take in strangers and give them protection is warranted for the people of Israel in the reminder that "you were strangers in Egypt." The memory of injustice suffered does not have to lead to fencing ourselves in and defending our property.

How asylum in churches is discussed in the church today depends on whether it is seen from "above" or "below." But, as Luise Schottroff has not only asserted but also demonstrates again and again, the Bible is and remains "our best ally."

MEMORIES OF HEINRICH BÖLL

Heinrich Böll is someone I sorely miss. Since his death in the summer of 1985, someone is missing whose presence was a refuge, someone who listened and said, "Don't put up with that," someone in whose stories I could hear sounds and smell odors, someone who could be silent and not send me away. I miss a man who hated war the way usually only women do and who can smell war in the most unpretentious denial or attenuation of the past or in the bureaucracy's most harmless military preparedness. I miss this someone who did not desert or emigrate, two options that in this country come readily to mind. The one I miss stayed, being at home neither in this country nor on this earth. I miss this someone, without whom it seems colder.

I remember one summer evening in the Eifel mountain region. We were sitting around a table outside; there were Hein and Annemarie Böll, one of their daughters-in-law, and us who had come from Cologne. Just as on other occasions we would get talking or even into debate, this evening we began singing. One song called forth another. Annemarie seemed to grow younger and younger—she remembered every verse. Singing came as naturally as eating food and drinking wine. Even though I was always sure that I was not a bit hungry, when we visited the Bölls I always ate; during the last years, when Hein affectionately and mockingly called me "old one," I would hear him say to me, "Have another glass of wine, old one."

The closeness that we came to take for granted had grown slowly. It was in Vilma Sturm's house in 1967 that I first met Böll. The Vietnam War was going on and we were all in a major process of conscientization in relation to the poor countries we soon came to call the "Third World." I remember visiting the Bölls on another occasion in their apartment on Belvedere Street; their place was crammed with that awful postwar furniture, but it felt marvelous that furniture could be so unimportant.

It must have been two or three years after we came to know one another when Hein proposed that we replace the formal "*Sie*" with the more personal pronoun "*du.*" In those days, this relationship-defining, familiar form of address was not nearly as customary as it is now. As if to test his own suggestion, Böll began with "Fulbert! Dorothee!" which made us very happy. Hein had a rare talent for gift-giving. It happened as easily as an affectionate touch, leaving no sense of embarrassment in the recipient. Awkward responses, such as "You shouldn't have . . . I can't accept this," became superfluous. His invitation often came in the form of "Come, visit us, we have time." These words of his were spoken in a world where all important people have no time; his words were an incidental gift, like the flowers he brought to our wedding, wrapped in brown paper.

To us in the circle of the Political Evensong in Cologne, Heinrich Böll was like a father. He was an internal touchstone by which we guaged our texts, a counselor in the endless conflicts with church bureaucracy and the police. His attentiveness as a listener was marked by spontaneous responses, such as "Those pigs" or simply, "Despicable, despicable." Böll supported the Evensong that since October 1968 took place monthly in Cologne, but he criticized our wish to conduct it, if possible, in a Roman Catholic church.

At that time, the Bölls were seeking to divert their church taxes to a congregation in Chico, Ecuador. Naturally, the vicar-general's office (from whom the tax money would be diverted) rejected the idea as an unreasonable demand. And so, the Bölls finally left the institution, feeling it was unworthy of trust, while we remained in it.

Besides at the demonstrations in Bonn, the capital of West Germany, and the blockade of the nuclear missile camp at Mutlangen, I encountered Heinrich Böll chiefly at events in the Cologne Cathedral. For example, in the fall of 1970, the issue was sixteen Basque freedom fighters whom Franco's Spain had condemned to die. With the Bölls the previous evening, we had devised a plan to hold an all-night vigil in the Cathedral. The term "occupation of the cathedral" did not originate with us, since we felt that it was "our cathedral" in which we gathered for prayer and protest a quarter of an hour before the doors were officially locked.

We prayed psalms that Ernesto Cardenal had recomposed. We listened to reports of torture, and we refused to be sent out of the cathedral. Finally we were locked in—Spaniards and Germans, people from the Republican Club and the Political Evensong.

During the subsequent protracted talks with the church administration, Böll played his part in a manner typical of Cologne: simultaneously cunning, appeasing, and pious. He tried to win over the church officials who at first simply did not get it. When two young people lit a cigarette, he entreated the horrified head of the cathedral chapter in the dialect of Cologne, "They don't know any better! You must explain this to them, really! These are people who simply don't know that you do not smoke in a church."

Later, the suffragan bishop came and tried to persuade us to go, citing—among other things—the lack of toilet facilities. Could we not come back and pray some other day? Even though the lives of the condemned were at stake right now, the bishop proposed the men's world day of prayer in a month's time, asking the Spaniards to return then. At that point Heinrich Böll said something that I will never forget. "But Bishop, you cannot postpone Gethsemane."

Gethsemane was now, the dark night in Cologne Cathedral. Some of us had wrapped ourselves in blankets, others were lying down on pews. I was eight months pregnant and eventually went home; Fulbert and Hein left with me and went for a drink at the railway station before going home. As a result of the worldwide protests, the condemned were pardoned two days later.

When a friend dies, an older brother, it feels at first like an amputation: a part of you is missing. Even though its presence was not something we were always aware of, the presence of its absence is something that is suddenly there all the time. People who have had an amputation tell of feeling pain where there is nothing. After experiencing this amputation, I feel the need to recall, to look at pictures, to say to friends, "Do you remember when . . . ?" I dig up things like that colorfully painted little wooden jar with soil from Russia in it. Hein gave it to our daughter Mirjam for her baptism, murmuring sheepishly, "They're possessed, those Russians . . . them and their soil," knowing full well that a child needs soil.

In addition to remembering, something else arises from my labor of mourning: The knowledge that I have become older, because no "grownup" is there to protect me anymore. Without noticing it, I have moved into the role of protecting others and, perhaps, that is an approach to death, a way of smiling sadly, like Heinrich Böll did. Smiling like that is something I would still like to learn.

WHEN HEINRICH BÖLL DIED

Who will protect me now
against the projectiles of the police
who fire into the unarmed crowd
Who protects my eyes
against the tear gas
Who protects our voices
against the gag of silence
Who shields our mind
against Boenisch & Company of the tabloid *Bild*
and who shields our heart
against despair
against turning cold

Who reminds us now
of the bread of early years
and of the taste of guilt
the smell of damp toggery
in a cramped apartment
and the sacrament of a cigarette shared
Who reminds us now
of this kind of love of the enemy
you spoke of as politeness

Who protects us now
from ourselves
Who comforts me
with comfortlessness
Who promises us
not victory under a sky
of ever more beautifully gleaming warplanes
but at least tears
Who strengthens us
with having no weapons
Who intercedes for us

BEING LEFTIST AFTER THE BIG CHANGE

After the collapse of communist rule in Eastern Europe, I was frequently asked whether that event did not—finally—also spell the end of socialism. It was with scarcely concealed glee that the end of all utopias, not only the Marxist one, was determined once and for all and the final triumph of capitalism proclaimed. The end of history was rung in with the American presidential advisor Francis Fukuyama. A postmodern day called to new shores.

I often fear that Christianity and socialism are hardly anything but dinosaurs in postmodernity. The postmodern world thoroughly disposes of every sort of Christian or socialist vision of humanity as so much obsolescence. There is no common good whereby human beings feel responsible for what happens in their village, or their part of the city, or to the neighbors and the children.

The new form of human development that is purged of compassion, the organizing of human beings perceived as "singles," consumerism as the aesthetic fulfillment of humankind: That is postmodernity. The dominant class looks on with a condescending smile. This is what the dynamic young entrepreneurs, the ranking executives and employees have left for the rest of us, whether we be humanists, socialists, or Christians. And I ask if it does not take a piece of religious language in order to safeguard a compassionate interrelationship among people, to keep commonality and a life that is good for all.

And so a question faces the community of the successors of those dreams for humanity. Can a place be found for its hopes within an utterly alternativeless capitalism? Can the beast be tamed, its claws clipped, and its cravings—for more cars and better weapons—be stilled? The victors' vision appears: "Everyone can be as well off as we are; those who don't succeed have no one to blame but themselves." Ecologically and economically, such a vision cannot be fulfilled on this earth; everyone knows that. And so our victorious right-wing intellectuals cut out the "everyone"; after all, who still dreams such stuff anyway? History capitulates to the perspective of the white males of the upper and middle classes in the rich countries for whom history has indeed reached a glorious climax. Those forever unchanging utopias, now labeled "dogmatic" and then "fanatical," only impede and upset a highly seductive pragmatism. Away, then, with the Sermon on the Mount and similar manifestos.

Mockery aside, the new situation after the big change calls for new reflection. Without self-criticism, the Left will hardly get out of its sulking corner to return from the retreat of injured silence it is in at the moment. The question is justified: What did we do wrong?

For an answer, one has to go far back in time. In the course of its history, Christianity has produced so many self-distortions and defeats that we, being used to grief, could show some more revolutionary patience. In connection with the quest for socialism after Stalinism, I want to name, as a Christian woman, my older experience. For 2,000 years there has existed a peculiar Christianity that burns witches at the stake, supports the *conquista*, invents the Inquisition, and creates oppression again and again. Nonetheless, I believe in Jesus Christ, in God, in hope, in humanity. I do so in a manner that acknowledges those terrible self-destructions. I do not try to evade them. It is my daily fare to meet people at every turn who have been disappointed, bent out of shape, even nauseated and destroyed by Christianity. They wonder what I still want to do with it.

Still, I think that the history of misuse cannot displace the usable past. So it is with socialism: We cannot and ought not bid it farewell, as if the principles and insights that have embodied themselves in that system of thought have been refuted by the fact that they were so terribly misused. But we do need a practical "dry cleaning" of those concepts and an alternative to state socialism. We can still show that socialism can go different ways, that other possibilities exist. But we must not let our critical analysis of systems be taken away from us, nor allow the alternative attempts that are now in process to be destroyed. There has to be a third way. For me it is simply unthinkable to accede to the banal logic of separatism: capitalism or Stalinism.

The historically necessary decline of communism is not the result of the agitation and craftiness of the West's anticommunism. Rather, it has everything to do with the authoritarianism and undemocratic character of state socialism and its unbearable mockery of human rights. We on the left have often relied on false modes of thinking and wondered whether one or another injustice of state socialism was not just a consequence of Western anticommunism. We tried to fight that anticommunism, but the failure of state socialism cannot be explained historically or economically in terms of it. The miserable statistics of productivity in the East horrified me and many of my friends in the German Democratic Republic (GDR); indeed, no one can evade a clear recognition and acknowledgment of this. That is why self-critical questions are so necessary: Where did we keep silent when we should have spoken out? Which elements of theory did we carry around without question, and where were we pie-eyed as far as developments in the GDR were concerned?

It was the civil rights movement of the GDR that posed these questions especially to the West German peace movement. For us—meaning my home-group, the Christian left—the collapse of authoritarian state socialism was not the end of our hopes. We were not interested in establishing conditions like those in the GDR. This stone-age and anticommunist allegation, no matter how many thousand times it has been repeated since 1989, is no more accurate now than it has been in forty preceding years. But the critical questions of some friends and companions do compel us to reflect. I am thinking of Bärbel Bohley or even Rainer Eppelmann, both of whom I visited in the '80s, constantly pursued by secret-service cars, which stood waiting just feet away from the homes of my dialogue partners.

The relationship between the peace movement and the human rights movement raised a central political question: Do they not belong inseparably one to the other? Why, in the West, did our quest for peace focus only on stopping the missiles? Did we not have to attack with equal passion the structures of injustice, the curtailing of the freedom of opinion, travel, education, and vocation, and other civil rights issues?

I had a different idea: I had hoped that reduced pressure from arms-modernization would result in a softening of conditions and allow gradual democratization. With many others, I hoped that more peace from without and more agitation for peace from within would bring both those goals closer; my experiences in the GDR confirmed this.

In the mid-'80s, I spoke in an overcrowded church in Dresden about "the arms race kills, even without war." (Later, it became a book with that title.) In the discussion afterward, one of the listeners passionately criticized state-socialist education. As a father, he spoke against an education that taught acquiescence and groveling before superiors; he did so with verve and great intelligence. The worst, he said, was that the young people are led into cynicism toward their own convictions. While he spoke, there was deathly silence in the overcrowded hall. Every word of his I could have spoken in my own context, but my stomach was gripped in fear. "Keep your mouth shut," I thought, "they'll come for you in a moment. They're just waiting for this." But nothing happened to the speaker. I learned later from friends that he was a well-known physician. They also told me that a whole series of spies from a state security "firm" had been in the church, as was customary. "What has changed?" I asked. "Fear has grown smaller," said the minister who had invited me. After the big change, I have often had cause to think about this experience. No one could anticipate how rapidly the end was going to come, but the signs of civil courage, independence of mind, and democratic candor were in the air.

I also took part in a meeting of a small ecology group in the parish hall. A physicist spoke about harmful substances in the air and contrasted them with the official reassurances. As before, I inquired later about the presence of the state security, the *Stasi*. "The woman who sat next to you has been a member of the group for four years. She has not spoken once. We assume that she is from 'the firm.'" Their courage and growing self-confidence amazed me.

Many of those engaged in the civil rights movement of the GDR were asking themselves whether they should stay in the country or leave. I was acquainted with the discussion of this matter in the church and had made my own the position that was identified by the words of the prophet Isaiah: "Whoever believes, remains." The church called on its co-workers not to go to the West, at least as a rule. Jeremiah's word, "Seek the welfare of the city," accompanied the church's admonition.

I remember a visit to a peace group in the city of Jena. The conversation among the eighteen people gathered in a living room began with a woman saying, in a somewhat rote fashion: "We who have decided to remain . . . " I did not know how to interpret that. After a while I understood what was behind those words. Several younger members of the group had intended to provoke the state authorities in such a manner that they would be deported to the West. Those who were staying behind were bitter about their behavior. They felt used by people who said "peace" but meant "getting out."

Naturally, I could not presume to pass judgment on this issue, but my sympathy was with those who remained. I had a wonderful conversation at that time with Christa and Gerhard Wolf, whom I met at a conference. After the big change, Christa Wolf became the victim of a smear campaign; she was attacked because, hoping for more democracy, she had remained.

Where did the critics in the newspaper feuilletons get the right to demand declarations of allegiance to capitalism?

One more issue of self-criticism on the part of the West's left was in relation to human rights. "Why do you always speak only of Chile, South Africa, or El Salvador? In our own land there is plenty of injustice that cries out to heaven! Why such one-eyed vision?" Such questions bothered me the most. Our excuse for this onesidedness was obvious: During the cold war, the Western media gladly took up every human rights violation in the Eastern bloc, while reports concerning violations by our allies in Pretoria, Washington, or Santiago de Chile were generally suppressed or doctored. Thus it seemed more important to us to show how, in our allegedly democratic system, human rights violations occurred at the margins, while at the center rights were relatively secure. In the process, what happened in the East was often lost from sight. A bitter aftertaste about our behavior lingers on.

But it is still this perspective on the whole world that determines what "being leftist after the big change" may mean. I consider it an inappropriate curtailment when human rights are defined now only in the Western sense. That the collective human rights to shelter and work, to potable water and breathable air, to medical attention and childcare are preserved or finally being established is something that cannot be relinquished—also and especially after the big change. What we had hoped for since Germany's reunification was that the jobless remaining third of women, the physically challenged, and other people might have work.

It was not the sulking corner, but much more the way people were afraid of that which I observed in many places and had me worried. I want to depict this in reference to part of the movement or mobilization of the last ten years. As I mentioned earlier, the Christian utopia was spoken of there as "the Conciliar Process" and was spelled out in the triad of "justice, peace, and integrity of creation." That concept signified that we now live not in "reconciliation," but in a kind of war on the poor, in a peace that secures itself only through terror, on course toward the iceberg that can indeed undo creation. That is the compelling prognosis. The Conciliar Process, which originated in the churches, insists on the dire need for a different global economic order, a peace based in justice and the "integrity of creation."

This process—it had a much more vibrant existence in the GDR, for good reasons—now appears to have dissipated. Even several years ago I heard Christian friends say that "the Conciliar Process is dead." I was so angry at this that I said to them: "It is you who are dead!" Can we imagine what it is to live without reconciliation? Enmity against children, fish, and butterflies turns into enmity against the cheerful, energetic, craving ego itself. The Bible called this enmity sin, separation from life; the community of those who continue to dream the Christian or socialist dream for humanity are not alone in finding that enmity intolerable. Much more was promised to everyone in this "incorruptible inheritance." (I apologize for so much use of Paul, but he is simply quite clear on this.) Everyone needs more than what postmodern identity offers to some. I am not worried for the long haul: No one can sterilize that community forever. We shall have children. Correction: No one can sterilize it except us ourselves.

Could a Christianity oriented toward the left not present an opposing power? The question makes me stammer. Part of the Christian churches moves toward such opposition at a snail's pace. I see such leaning, for example, in the Pastoral Letters of the U.S. Catholic bishops, whom one might already call moderately social-democratic. I see it as well in the church assembly or *Kirchentag* in Germany, in its broad openness to developing countries and the Conciliar Process, its awakening to a new spirituality that acts like a counterprogram to the fundamentalists' sectarian piety. But how very slowly it moves forward theologically! However, I am not without hope, to put it cautiously. I feel more sustained today than twenty years ago, borne by a broader stream in the *oekumene* by Christians committed to peace, justice, and the protection of creation and seeking to turn those three foci of the Conciliar Process into issues of politics.

And even though it is not very trendy these days, *"Ich steh hier und singe/In gar sichrer Ruh."* ("*I stand here and sing/In most serene calm.*" Bach enthusiasts may hum the verses before and after about the raging, crashing "world.") Or, as Pablo Neruda put it, "For now I demand no more than the right to eat." Does anyone seriously believe that we could live without hunger and thirst for justice?

LEARNING TO FLY

Theology and literature are a *cantus firmus,* a leading theme in my life. In my judgment, the two have to be in relation one to the other. I examined the relation in a formal, scholarly manner in my habilitation dissertation which was published as a book in 1973 and titled *Realization: Studies in the Relation between Theology and Fiction since the Enlightenment.* The study originated in my theological interest in literature. My interest was aroused by the numerous traces of religious language in fiction-writing that does not regard itself as religious at all; I refer to quotations from and allusions to the Bible and to figures and motifs, images and personalities of the world of religion. In the course of a process of secularization, the language of Christian faith has come to be at the disposition of indirect, metaphorical speech and has taken on most diverse functions anywhere between blasphemy and sacralization.

It is the emancipative use of religious language in fiction-writing that justifies not only the theologian's but also the literary scholar's asking about the theological implications of such acceptance and appropriation. What role does the linguistic domain of the Bible or of general religiosity play in a text constructed in accordance with different rules? For what did the writer need that linguistic domain? What part does theology then have in the different text? What perspective did it bring to that text? On what can a theological interpretation base itself, and what would it look like? Such were my questions as I studied interpretations of the writings of Georg Büchner, William Faulkner, Thomas Mann, Karl Philipp Moritz, Jean Paul, and Alfred Döblin.

A few years before, Peter Hammer Verlag took on an experiment, an annual on literature and theology, edited by Wolfgang Fietkau, Armin Juhre, Kurt Marti, and me. Beginning in 1967, it was published for fifteen years. Among its general topics were death in society, violence, revolution and love, fear, the male, marriage, alternative living. The editorial meetings were great fun; I remember them with real pleasure.

Poetry, religion, and politics sustain damage whenever they are separated from each other, existing in spiritual apartheid. My friend Kurt Marti devotes himself to controlling the damage that the lack of poetry has inflicted on the theology of the academy. The beauty of theology, its seriousness and its playfulness, is made visible in his work (as it is, by the way, in my husband's essays and books). This kind of poetry is no luxury item; it is bread. It turns our planet, ever so beloved in spite of everything, more and more into home.

The separation of the domains of aesthetics, politics, and religion is the dogma of modernity that I could never completely agree to. An allegedly politics-free religion ends up venerating power and its idols, whereas poetry creates a boundary-dissolving freedom, a kind of oceanic feeling. I really do not believe in the modern program of *poésie pure*: Wherever it happens successfully that the unmixed purity of the beautiful becomes sound and language, poetry is no longer "pure" and "for itself." Paul Celan's lyrical work serves as an example of how precisely, in most sparse, often hermetic language, the reality of the world of the extermination camp enters and the promises of tradition shine forth.

When I learned Greek, the concept *kalonkagathon* became very dear to my heart. In my seventeen-year-old unintelligence, I wondered how the Greeks could take two words that for us have nothing to do with each other, and turn them into the one word: beauty-good. Where on earth would one find aesthetics and ethics in the same dish? My amazement was deepened even more when I found out that medieval theology taught that God touches us through beauty, changes us, and draws us Godward. This thought meets us in many a tradition of mysticism, including those of Islam; it has taken deep root in me now. In order really to do theology, we need a different language. Poetry and liberation are topics central to my life. Something is lacking when, for an extended period of time, I have written no poetry.

I try to say in poems what annoys me and what gives me joy, what makes me suffer and what comforts me. In more recent literature, there is a great deal of self-pity; and I find that disquieting, because I find that one needs to praise God, if such pious language is at all appropriate. Without giving praise, we do not really breathe. And the only way of sharing the experience of liberation is by naming what is good and freeing. Meister Eckhart puts it as follows: *"Gott ist das Allermitteilsamste."* ("God is all-sharing.") Why is it often so impossible to share God?

The titles of my books of poems speak of blessedness: "Learning to Fly," "Crazy about Light," and "Play Something about Bread and Roses."

For me it is like taking a breath, as well as an imperative, to speak of something besides misfortune. It is the experience of hearing and the process of speaking that govern my poetry writing. I try to work on linguistic precision and conviction.

The German writer Friedrich Gottlieb Klopstock (1724–1803) wrote beautifully about religion and poetry. "There are ideas that can hardly be expressed except in poetry; or, rather, it is appropriate to the nature of certain subjects to reflect on them poetically and to make clear that too much would be lost were they to be thought about in any other way. In my judgment, contemplations on God's omnipresence belong essentially in this category." It strikes me that Klopstock is pleading for a bit of pantheism here. The presence of God can be articulated neither in the language of everydayness, of triviality, nor of science.

When one tries to communicate God, that is, to say something that goes beyond the language of everyday life, one has to search. Unlike many theologians who actually want to do scholarship, my own search does not take the scholarly path. I do not believe that searching that way will lead us on. Instead, I believe that theology is much more an art than a science. It has to understand itself as an attempt to cross the bounds of everyday language, oriented toward art rather than to the abstract, rational, and neutral. Why is it that in the world of the West only theology developed and not theopoetry?

The endeavor to communicate God does not lead me away from reality, or from images to levels of abstraction. I try to think in images and, even more so, in stories, in narratives. In this respect, I have always learned much from Judaism. Often I have experienced what it means to have a discussion with Jewish people. There always comes a point when they interrupt their argumentation and exclaim, accompanied by an inimitable gesture, "Now, I will tell you a story." Jewish interpretation of Scripture works in much the same way; it is not oriented toward doctrinal assertions but toward application, toward wisdom for living.

I have often narrated events in poetry, framing and preserving information that was important to me. The narrative element has a poetic magic for me:

> And I saw a man on 126th Street
> broom in hand
> sweeping eight feet of the street
> Meticulously he removed garbage and dirt

from a tiny area
in the midst of a huge expanse
of garbage and dirt

And I saw a man on 126th Street
sorrow sat on his back
sweeping eight feet of the street
Wear and tear showed on his arms
in a city
where only crazy folk
find something to hope in

And I saw a man on 126th Street
broom in hand
There are many ways to offer prayer
With a broom in the hand
is one I had hitherto
not seen before

For me, praying and writing poetry, prayer and poem, are not alternatives. The message I wish to pass on is meant to encourage people to learn to speak themselves. For example, the idea that every human being can pray is for me an enormous affirmation of human creativity. Christianity presupposes that all human beings are poets, namely, that they can pray. That is the same as seeing with the eyes of God. When people try to say with the utmost capacity for truthfulness what really concerns them, they offer prayer and are poets at the same time. To discover this anew, to bring it into reality or to make it known, is one of the goals I pursue in my poems.

When I have spent time with someone and have been touched by particular points in our conversation, I often feel the need to write it down and to reconstruct or clarify it for myself. It is as if I experience the conversation all over again, in a more intense way. It must have something to do with the fact that I like to deepen my relationship with the now, the present. In other words, I seek to live truly now; I don't want to defer life to a future, more joy-filled condition. I want to learn to take what is here now, to see and hear it, which is to say, to live more attentively. Attentiveness has become an important concept for me particularly on account of Simone Weil's ideas on the subject. To be attentive also in everyday occurrences and to listen, to inquire, and to interpret attentively in a conversation—this is what makes for a poem.

I experience our language as broken, horribly corrupted. When the word "love" gets applied to a car, or the word "purity" to detergents, then these words have lost all meaning; they have been stolen. In this sense, all words among us that express feelings have sustained serious damage. This is especially true for the language of religion. "Jesus Christ is our redeemer"—this is destroyed, dead language. It means absolutely nothing, no one understands it; it is religious babble that, although available in staggering quantity, no longer says anything. This is what I mean when I say that language is broken.

Let me tell about an opposite incident. My five-year-old granddaughter Johanna came home from kindergarten and said: "What happened to Jesus was very bad; they made him dead with nails through his hands. But then, there was Easter and, ha-ha, he got up again." For that happily spontaneous "ha-ha," I would gladly give away several yards of exegetical literature.

I believe that a good dose of despair about the old language, a portion of disgust, is part of writing. That is a very natural sensation. Shame is a revolutionary sensation, Karl Marx once said. One has to be ashamed of and suffer from the twaddling that goes on, how language is being destroyed, how human beings are being destroyed or cannot recognize themselves anymore in what is being spoken. In such shame, I move toward something in order to find the language that is perhaps already present somewhere. For example, I find much in the language of the Bible; there I find rather than produce. I would not like to live without the Psalms and much less without finding my own psalm, even if it is as short as Johanna's "ha-ha." It is important that people make their own pains clear to themselves, articulate their own questions in a greater depth, and express more accurately that they are . . . learning to fly.

THE DEATH OF MY MOTHER

My mother died in September 1990; she had turned eighty-seven that year. The last nine nights and eight days I spent at her deathbed in my parents' house in Cologne. At first she did not recognize me but held my hands very tightly with her lean, bony hands. She would gesticulate, utter deep sighs, or call out loudly for "Mama," "Papa," "Strasbourg," the city of her birth, and sometimes for her grandchildren, my children. When I stood by her, I began to say whatever came into my head. "It won't be much longer. It is a dark tunnel you have to go through; it is bright on the other side. Don't be afraid, I am staying with you now. The tunnel is awful, very narrow, but then there is space and light."

I thought then of how often my mother, who had given birth to five children, had compared death to the exertions and pains of birth. It was a thought that seemed to calm her: Death is work that has to be completed. I did not know whether she took in any of my words; my touch and my quiet but firm voice clearly gave her calm.

Then it occurred to me to sing to her, because words no longer carried my intention. I sang "Commit Thy Ways to God," a hymn of the church she had liked. One of my daughters had recited it when Mother had her eightieth birthday. I sang the three or four verses that I knew by heart and added other hymns, as well as liturgical responses like the "*Laude omnes gentes, laudate dominum*" from Taizé. When I could not remember how it continued, I would hum the melody once again, loudly and clearly. My mother grew calmer and fell asleep.

In the following nights and days, I sang to her for many hours. I bought a hymnbook and read the verses I was missing. I discovered how many hymns include dying in their texts, even when they are about the dawning morning or the forests at rest. When I came to a verse with these lines: "The body hurries now to rest, take off the garment and the shoes, the image of mortality," my mother nodded and stretched her feet. How often had she felt at ease when she had kicked off her shoes! I could not know whether she heard or even believed the continuation of that verse,

"Those I take off but Christ will clothe me with the gown of honor and glory."

Everything I sang seemed to me to be connected. Her feet had turned blue and were swollen, but Paul Gerhardt, the hymn writer, had more than that to say about the feet of my mother: "The One who gives air and wind their course and path will find paths where your feet may tread." She who later cried out for air heard the word "air" very clearly.

Far more direct than my prose was the language of hymns that were often related to memories of other people. I also sang the sentimental hymn "Take Now My Hands," in memory of my godmother, a deaconess at the Bethel Institutes. She had died well over fifty years ago, the first dead person I had knowingly seen as a child. The lines "Wrap me 'round wholly with your mercy," called up for us—or who knows, only for me—the great blanket of evening, night, and death.

What was I doing? I invited the dead, whom my mother had loved, to be present; I spoke the name of my brother who had died while a prisoner of war. With the dead, the past returned. I also sang about the gentle moon that so quietly drifted through the clouds of evening, a song my mother had sung to her great-grandchild because of the tender lines, "Beam lovingly into the quiet chambers of those in sorrow."

My mother was a child of the nineteenth century, even though friends sometimes styled her as a lady of the seventeenth century. Her relation to church and piety was a formal one; during her final years, it was even cool. She would distance herself from religion and faith with the rote response: "We don't know that." It astonished me how often she folded her hands during a nearly four-weeks-long death struggle. As if crying out loud were not enough.

Every now and then I also recited a Psalm, the 23rd, about the good shepherd, and 126, "When the Lord will release Zion's imprisoned, we shall be like you who dream." Yet it almost seemed as if the foreign tones of the Latin prayers touched her more deeply. While singing to her, I had a feeling of being connected to her, as if she had found contentment through it. It did not seem as if I were doing something "for her," but as if we were together walking toward something greater than we are. An old theological conviction of mine was strengthened during those nights at her deathbed, namely, that without mutuality, without giving and taking on both sides, there can be no love. God cannot "give" us anything if we do not become the bearers and givers of God's power.

The singing and praying that are still alive in the culture of Catholic villages help both those who actively take part in their dying and those who are with them during the time of transition. I sang, "Swing Low, Sweet Chariot," as much for Mother as for myself, "coming for to carry me home," as if we all stood at the Jordan where Christ had replaced the ancient, sullen ferryman, Charon.

The physician and several members of the family had often announced that her death was near. And for a whole year of illness, how much I had wished that it would come! She herself had often told an anecdote about the death of President Hindenburg: He asked his physician Sauerbruch, "Professor, is friend Hein in the room yet?" and was told, "No, your Excellency, but at the door." In such stories, she expressed that she was preparing herself for death; indeed, she signaled, albeit rather late, more and more clearly her wish to die.

But energy to live was stronger than her conscious awareness. She still wanted to do so much—to sit up, get more air, be turned over, get a drink. A whole day long she called out, "Turn over!" in tones of complaint, command, and adjuration, as if words like "help," "Mama," "turn over," and "out" were about one and the same purpose, even though assigned to different days. Often she left language well behind and would answer only by shaking her head or nodding. The movements of her arms and hands had become smaller.

The first evening with her, I could hardly complete the verse "When my time comes to leave," because of my tears. The last evening, I was able to sing it calmly. When I came to the lines "Come and let me see you, be my comfort as I die," I thought about the many different images that arise during dying, of being left alone in childhood or in fear.

The names of her grandchildren came to Mother more often than those of her own children. Are we to cling to images, such as that of the light at the end of the tunnel? Are they needed—by us who die passively or by those who actively seek death? If death is the absolute condition without images, is it possible to outfit it with images and thus to humanize it? Can death come, as Matthias Claudius—and Schubert—put it, "as friend, not for punishment"?

The final hymn I sang was "Lord, Have Mercy." My mother had again begun to breathe steadily, albeit rapidly. I had put my hand on hers; her face was completely without tension. Her last sigh was quite light, like an astonished "ah." For a moment, I doubted that the long awaited had arrived. But it had stepped into the room.

MY BEST FRIEND

To use the language of children, Luise Schottroff is my "best friend." We had become superficially acquainted during the '60s, in the circle of pupils and friends of Rudolf Bultmann, the "Old Marburgers," who gathered every autumn. The few women who showed up there were essentially held to be peripheral figures. Together with Marie Veit and another woman-theologian, I once tried to propose to this venerable circle that it change its policy regarding invitations. The result was that Ernst Fuchs, professor of New Testament in Marburg, walked out, highly insulted.

Toward the end of the '60s, the years of student unrest long behind us, Luise and I were drawn into our first major conflicts with the institutions of church and university. Having successfully completed her habilitation in the winter term of 1968–69, Luise applied for the position in New Testament, vacated by the retirement of Herbert Braun at the University of Mainz. She had the enthusiastic support of the student body; the professional veto scuttled her application. The students protested by occupying the dean's offices. An important part in the conflict was played by a proposed reform of the universities that envisaged one-third of those participating in decision-making to be students. We were nowhere near such a reform in 1971 when my first attempt to be granted habilitation failed; the old Faculty of Philosophy, consisting of about sixty men, decided entirely on its own.

The friendship between Luise and me grew as a part of our experience of conflict. Seen from today's perspective, there are three points that seem to be especially important to me in the growth of our friendship: distancing ourselves from the existing academic theology, the emergence of a new understanding of spirituality, and our entry into the women's movement.

Our respect for German university theology began to fall apart. Not only was that theology removed from praxis, it even prided itself on *not* having a praxis, that is to say, it gave its blessing to a false one. In this it was in complete contrast to what was happening in the ecumenical churches. This became very apparent to Luise in Mainz, when the anti-racism program of the World Council of Churches was discussed in the theological section of the university there in 1969. Resistance against the courageous and far-sighted program to combat racism came from professors who were also members of synods. We asked ourselves not only how they understood the Bible, but also what they believed in at all.

It is not far-fetched to fix the moment when social-historical interpretation of Scripture was born within this context. Here, as in the Political Evensong in Cologne, it had been less the student movement of 1968 that caused us to critique established theology than our own reflection within Christianity.

This leads into the second point I mentioned. I recall an incident in an association organized by professors, Braun, Mezger, and Otto, from Mainz. I argued that, on the basis of my experiences with the Political Evensong, "a new piety" was needed. The majority of the leftist-liberal theologians of the circle of Gert Otto took that to be a kind of pietistic throwback, unworthy of an enlightened spirit. Analysis? Yes. Critique of existing conditions? Yes. Structural change? Yes. But piety? Who needs it, and who profits from it?

In vain I tried to make the case in light of the understanding my radicalized Roman Catholic friends were presenting. Finally, Bernd Paschke intervened; he later worked in Latin America. He built a bridge by suggesting that what I meant by that impossible concept, "becoming more radical and more pious," is what in French is called *spiritualité*. At the time, that word was not yet part of my active vocabulary. But the tension between a secular—today one would say "post-Christian"—critique, and what later came to be known as the liberation theology stance became very apparent.

I remember so vividly that I was worried about where Luise would take her stand in this fundamental decision. Later she would often speak of it in terms of "conversion" to the power of tradition, to the necessity of rereading Scripture, to hope even in times when the empirical basis of hope seems ever so thin—in other words, conversion to worship and prayer.

And when did feminism finally begin to move you? some may ask with some impatience. It was stalled by a historical, bourgeois delay! When asked in those years whether the discrimination we experienced almost every day in church and academy had anything to do with our being women, we most often replied, "Actually, no." It had to do with our comments on the Vietnam War and perhaps also with our notion that God does not act from on high by pushing a heavenly button but, instead, in and with us.

We named political and theological reasons why we—each in her own way—were rendered invisible, excluded from the curriculum or suspected of being "unscholarly." It took some time, and many sisters, before we came to recognize sexism as one—or *the*—place where the false theology, the false structure of the university, the false ordering of life is to be broken open. The process of feminization of consciousness took a long time. It was no less dangerous than the one of searching for new forms of piety in which our fears, but also our untamed expectations, could express themselves and would stay alive.

Luise Schottroff, the teacher of New Testament and feminist liberation theologian, helped me learn to read the Bible with rigor and enthusiasm and to wrest it from the "Scripture thieves," about whom Thomas Müntzer had already spoken in the early sixteenth century. Above all, she taught me to use the Bible. She laughed with me when men strutted about all too arrogantly; she cried with me when the fish were dying in the Rhine. Her Prussian realism looked with some indignation on my spiritual excursions, and my Rhenish joie de vivre aroused her suspicion. Her perseverance has again and again rooted me in this land of our mothers.

Over the years, our friendship has grown deeper. Suspicion and lightheartedness have jostled each other, hiking and swimming have competed with one another. Luise's eyes for the plastic arts are sharper than mine. I like to close my eyes so as to be all ears. We have written three books together (one of them with Bärbel von Wartenberg), and I hope that it does not end there. Perhaps Luise's sober judgment will someday embrace my mysticism more. Perhaps I will learn with Lydia's sisters to wash the ugly stains off our inheritance.

In the past few years, we have both experienced illness, weakness, aging, and the one who lurks behind them ready to devour us. Once, when I was very ill, Luise visited me twice in the hospital; on one of these occasions I did not even know that she was there. When I heard about it later, my first reaction was, "What did she want here, seeing that I could not hear or feel?" But suddenly it dawned on me that her coming had been a gratuitous act, one of life's gifts, like the rose blossom, without a reason. I think friendship is when, almost naturally and sometimes without knowing it, we praise God.

BECOMING LIGHTER

When I climb stairs at my slow pace, I realize that I have become older; I am afraid of slowing down. When I cannot jump, I become impatient with myself. That is because I am brisk and feel a certain affection for everything that is agile, like mountain streams, little girls skipping rope.

I ask myself, how does one go about living more slowly, having time, becoming lighter? I would like to learn a bit more about that and find another relationship with time. At the moment, growing old means for me that my impatience grows with me. I hope that I may still learn to deal with this without entirely losing myself in the phenomenon of feeling ill or weak. That the rest of life will consist of that alone is, I believe, what I fear the most. It is terrible on occasion to observe this loss of self. I can imagine taking my own life, and I find it conceivable to go to that extreme; it does not conflict with my religious convictions. The continuation of life provided through technology and under whose edict we live goes against the will of life itself, against creation. Cleaving to life, or being chained to it without being asked, is morbid and artificial; life is then taken as a possession and not as something on loan to us for a period.

In my judgment, overcoming the technologism also of death is an assertion of freedom. I do not mean to convey that somehow I feel superior to life. There is a beautiful saying among Canada's indigenous peoples: "I heard the owl call my name." It means that when you hear the owl, you leave the village and go alone into a cabin out in the wilderness. There you die; that is, you relinquish food and being cared for. That is surely not pleasant, but I find a greater dignity to dying there than in what our culture has now produced.

I believe in the life after death, the life that goes on after my individual death. I believe in the peace that perhaps is to be some time long after I have gone, in justice and in joy. I do not believe in a continuation of individual existence, and I do not wish to be in a situation where I would have to believe in it. I regard such a belief to be a crutch for faith; we are, instead, to learn to walk and I want to learn to walk without having to rely on this bourgeois crutch.

If I had the faith of an Isaiah or Jeremiah, I would be satisfied; I do not need what Friedrich Nietzsche once called Christianity, "Platonism for the people," but I do need faith in the one who elects, liberates, and walks beside us. A young woman once asked me, "Is everything over for you when you die?" I replied that it all depends on what she meant by "everything." If you are "everything" to yourself, then everything is over for you. But if not, then everything goes on, as a beautiful Yiddish song puts it: "*mir leben ejbik*" ("we live eternally").

Individual spiritual, psychic, and somatic existence comes to an end at death. That idea does not fill me with fright that I am a part of nature, that I fall like a leaf from a tree and decay while the tree and the grass go on growing, the birds sing, and I am a part of all that. I am at home in this cosmos without having to go on living that piece of the whole that was mine for perhaps seventy years.

I find that we can learn much from the religions of East Asia that have seen very clearly that the whole is larger than its parts and that each one of us is a part. Those religions have fostered trust in the whole. Paul Tillich once formulated this very beautifully; he called it "the courage to confirm one's finitude," that is, to comprehend "I am finite, I will die," without having to despair because of it.

The best thing that I have learned concerning these matters has come from some letters by persons who had been condemned to die. Many of those people have died with dignity and freedom and not as the "*homo incurvatus in se ipsum*" ("the human being utterly twisted and turned in on the self"), as Luther used to depict the sinner. The redeemed sinner, the pardoned human being, has been set free from such self-encirclement.

In this context, I recall the writer Erich Fried, who died in November 1988. My friends Frieder and Sabine Stichler from Frankfurt, in whose house Erich Fried stayed every time he came to Frankfurt, allowed me to participate in Fried's long, drawn-out dying. On account of his openness and his absolute disregard for the line between the private and the public, Fried was "a member of the family" for many people, a man who belonged to them because he took an interest in everything. Here was a man of laughter and of weeping (even in public!), flirtation and loving, a man of all seasons with an incredible capacity for friendship, undivided attentiveness, and affection.

In 1985, Fried and I drove together by car to a public lecture; I asked Erich about his meeting with the young neo-Nazi, Michael Kühnen. He reported in great detail about the meeting and with heightened concern, almost as if he were amazed at himself. Their conversation on television had begun with the question how he imagined a neo-Nazi, to which he had replied that such a person perhaps plays soccer, goes to work, falls in love. In other words, Fried tried to do what he had always tried to do as a writer, to liberate from cliché and to put a human face back on those whom we are told to hate.

Thereupon Kühnen asked Erich Fried to visit him in prison. The already deathly ill writer goes and invites the young man to address him by his first name. When Kühnen claims that the story of those six million murdered Jews could not be true, Fried reacts without anger. He cites no statistics. Rather, he tells the young man about his grandmother. She had lived in Vienna and was taken to Terezin (Theresienstadt) and never returned. I assume that Erich explained to Michael Kühnen that he loved his grandmother, just as in poetry and prose he explained it to his readers.

This story of enlightenment between an old antifascist and a young neo-Nazi has peculiar features. How could someone as astute as Erich Fried count so idealistically and blindly on the reasonableness and humanity of someone this deluded? Perhaps "enlightenment" is too weak a word for what Fried did. He wanted more: He wanted to help this human being to show some mercy to himself, he wanted to convert him. To put it theologically: I know next to no one who distinguishes so clearly between sinner and sin. However much Erich Fried hated the sin, he was almost completely incapable of hating the sinner. Perhaps this incorrigible feature of Erich Fried's was what was most Jewish about him. Jewish tradition teaches about *teshuvah*, repentance, that there is no day and no hour in which it is not possible to turn back.

Some months later, we talked about Ingeborg Drewitz, the German writer who had died of cancer. Erich Fried faded away in his armchair and hid his head; it was not a collapse but a submerging. He wept. He envied Ingeborg in how she had handled her cancer. "I would still like to learn that," he said, resurfacing.

His awareness of dying got under my skin during another encounter. He had invited a number of writers to come to Wiesbaden to read from their works; many were younger and less renowned. We met on November 18, 1987; Fried presided, introduced, and participated. I read a poem titled "Four o'clock at night." It begins with the words, "Do come to me, angel of the sleepless" and ends with the lines:

> Angel of the sleeping I call you now for hours
> put your dark cover over my eyes strained from waking
> do come to me
> and greet the other angel
> your darker brother

There was a pause, because I assume the audience had not understood the ending—except for Erich Fried. He applauded spontaneously. For a time he and I were quite alone among the other guests, with that other angel.

It was the last time that I saw Erich Fried. But there was one more, different encounter that made me very happy. Three months later he telephoned. "This is Erich Fried. I am calling from London, and I only wanted to tell you that you absolutely must go on writing poems." I had voiced my doubts about the genre of the political poem—about which many of us had learned most from Brecht. I wondered, whom do I reach, and what changes from knowing more? We talked awhile, about cancer—his small one, and the big one of the arms race, about Nicaragua, about what we need poems for.

In that conversation he fought death without crying; later he wept openly. His fighting was filled with fear and with an ever new readiness to stand up against the fear of others and against the fearmongers; he fought without resigning. And yet, at the end, he was able to say, "Now I can die." Here was a teacher whom some young people look for and to whom they say: From you I want to learn to see, hear, taste, and speak this wholly indestructible love for life.

DON'T FORGET THE BEST

Thirteen years ago, when I became a grandmother for the first time, I had the feeling that this new role—grown by now to include three grandchildren—would surely make growing older easier for me. And I became aware once again that I still wanted to hand on something of what was important for my generation. I do not want my people to forget fascism. Theodor W. Adorno once said, "The very first demand of education is that Auschwitz does not happen once again."

I don't want to let go of this basic feeling, and I cannot do so. To the last I resist that this German event be leveled out, as for example in the *Historikerstreit*. I resist people's now talking as if this event could be relativized through comparison with other peoples who behaved no differently. I find the whole white-washing of the event simply unbearable. It is in this sense that I really struggle against getting older, and I declare: There are things that must not be forgotten! Remembering, collective remembering, is not a luxury but the indispensable key to liberation.

This is something that I, as an older person, wish to pass on: Do not forget! Only they who remember have a future and hope. I see myself as a link in a chain, as a wave in a large wave-pattern; I am not the whole thing, I am a part. Not that I bear the root: The root bears me, as Paul writes in Rom. 11:18. That calms me. There is a saying from the German Peasant Wars: "We go home beaten, the grandchildren will fare better." Ernst Bloch liked to quote these words. What is noted here is a connection between remembrance and the future; being beaten and seeing justice defeated are not in vain.

I remember an Irish fairy tale about the terrible trials a person must undergo when courting a prince or princess. "The king's son, who had just become my friend, must clean out a stable that has been manure-filled for 120 years. Every time he throws out one shovelful, three shovelfuls of smelly manure come flying back in through each of the forty wide-open windows."

As I understand it, what is the origin of theology? I believe that it really does take its rise in a stable that reeks of historic injustice. And there we are with our far too small spades, talking to one another. Theology that is truly alive never arises outside of and apart from its situation; it does not drop straight from heaven as "God's Word." Rather, it constitutes itself in the solidarity of those affected.

I continue to understand faith as a mixture of trust and fear, hope and doubt—in the Gospels Jesus called it great or little faith—as life's intensity, the search for the true prince and for the reign of God. A conversation, in the full sense of the word, comes into being when people share together their hunger for spirit in leaden, spiritless times. The satiated have no need to talk to each other.

My life is that of a theological worker who tries to tell something of God's pain and God's joy. My language has perhaps become "more pious," but it was not my subjective development alone, as I have tried to describe it here, that has led to this. It was my participation in the worldwide Christian movement toward a Conciliar Process in which justice, peace, and the integrity of creation finally, clearly represent the heart of faith. Theologically speaking, I think I am less alone today than years ago. To be able to say so is a kind of bliss: *¡Gracias a Dios!*

It was 1990 when a German radio station invited a contribution from me for one of its broadcast series; I was to compose a letter to my children and to state "what really counts in life." Grown-ups were to pass on what gave them comfort, what should not be forgotten or become lost. The following little text was my response:

Dear Children,

In the sagas and fairy tales I used to tell you years ago, there is a motif of a poor shepherd who one day is led far away by a little gray man, to a mysterious mountain. The mountain bursts open, and inside glisten the most precious treasures. But as the shepherd keeps stuffing his pockets, a voice calls out, "Don't forget the best!" The story goes on that the door crashes shut behind the shepherd, and the treasures in his pockets turn into dust.

I have never understood what "the best" was really supposed to be. Was it perhaps the clump of flowers at the gate of the mountain? Or a homely old lamp like that of Aladdin? Was it perhaps the key with which to get back in? Perhaps the wish to go back and not to forget?

Don't forget the best! All four of you know that the voice of the little gray man enticed me far away from ordinary life into religion, away from "its cultured despisers" and ever closer to something perhaps more Jewish than a dogmatic Christian faith. Of all the things I would have liked to give you in the midst of the enmity that life shatters you with, this is the most difficult to explain. I can't simply sign my treasures over to you. To love God with the whole heart, with all one's strength, from one's entire soul—and that in a world that breaks with tradition after tradition—is something I cannot pass on like an inheritance.

My attempts to raise you as Christians had little chance of succeeding; the institution again and again attacked me from behind, the church was and is only rarely worthy of trust. But I am also very conscious of my own lack of credibly living out customs and symbols, of making hymn and prayer part of everyday life. It is as if we parents had no house of religion to offer you to live in but a derelict one.

A visible manifestation of the difficulty that children with vitality have with their parents today is the fact that you, Mirjam, as the youngest, did not become confirmed. Yet you live no farther away from the treasure mountain and perhaps also hear the voice of the little gray man. That may have been the reason why I held back from enticing you into Christianity—the word "educate" is surely quite out of place in this situation.

But—organized religion or not—I *do* wish that you all become a little bit pious. Don't forget the best! I mean, that you praise God sometimes, not always—only the chatterers and the courtiers of God do so—but on occasion, when you are very happy, so that happiness flows by itself into gratitude and you sing "hallelujah" or the great *om* of Indian religion.

On our trips we used to drag you into churches; on one occasion, the church we looked at was awful. I believe it was you, Caroline, who announced dryly, "No God in there." Precisely that is not to be said in your lives; God is to be "in there," at the sea and in the clouds, in the candle, in music, and, of course, in love.

Without grounding in the ground of life, this true joy is not there, and our joy is then focused always on occasions and things. True joy, the joy of life, the happiness of being alive is not the joy that arises because there are strawberries, because school was canceled, or a wonderful visitor had arrived. True joy is without a "why," or as my best friend from the Middle Ages, Meister Eckhart, used to say, *"sunder warumbe"* ("utterly devoid of why").

If I could give you only a little of this *sunder warumbe* joy, strong mother or not, it would already be very much. Then I would readily let go of my unwelcome extra-special wishes, those motherly demands, such as that once in your life you would read Meister Eckhart: I would gladly turn back again into the little gray man and sit in the blue cave among the glistening jewels and call out, "Don't forget the best!"

Your old Mama

CHRONOLOGY

Sept. 30, 1929	Dorothee Nipperdey is born in Cologne, after brothers Carl, Otto, and Thomas, and before sister Sabine. Primary and secondary education in Cologne, interrupted by forced relocation during the war
1949–51	Studies in philosophy and ancient languages in Cologne and Freiburg
1951	Change to studies in Protestant Theology and German in Göttingen
1954	Graduation. Marriage to painter Dietrich Sölle. Doctoral dissertation in literary criticism, "Studies in the Structures of Bonaventura's Vigils"
1954–60	Instructor of Religion and German at the High School (Gymnasium) for Girls in Cologne-Mülheim
1956	Birth of son, Martin
1957	Birth of daughter, Michaela
1960–65	Freelance writer on theological and literary subjects for radio and serials
1961	Birth of daughter, Caroline
1962–64	Assistant at the Philosophical Institute of the Technical University of Aachen
1964	Marriage to Dietrich Sölle ends in divorce.
1964–67	Director of Studies at the Institute of German Studies of the University of Cologne
1968–72	Political Evensong in Cologne
1969	Marriage to Fulbert Steffensky, former Benedictine priest
1970–present	Member of P.E.N. of the Federal Republic of Germany
1970	Birth of daughter, Mirjam
1971	Habilitation at the University of Cologne
1972–1975	Sessional Instructor at the Faculty of Protestant Theology at the University of Mainz
1974	Awarded the Theodor-Heuss Medal

1975–87	Professor of Systematic Theology at Union Theological Seminary, New York, N.Y.
1977	Doctor of Theology *honoris causa*, Protestant Faculty, Paris
1981	Fellowship of the Lessing Prize, Hamburg
1982	Droste Prize for Lyric Poetry of the City of Meersburg
Aug. 6, 1985	Hiroshima Day civil disobedience action outside the Pershing II missile base at Mutlangen. Found guilty of "provoking arrest"
1987–88	Visiting Professor at the University of Kassel
1988	Sit-down action for peace outside the gates of the U.S. poison gas depot at Fischbach. Found guilty of "attempting to provoke arrest"
1991–92	Visiting Professor at the Faculty of Protestant Theology, University of Basel
1994	Named Honorary Professor of the University of Hamburg

BOOKS IN ENGLISH

Christ the Representative: An Essay in Theology after the Death of God. David Lewis, trans. Philadelphia: Fortress Press, 1967.

Suffering. Everett R. Kalin, trans. Philadelphia: Fortress Press, 1975.

Revolutionary Patience. Rita and Robert Kimber, trans. Maryknoll: Orbis Books, 1977.

Death by Bread Alone: Texts and Reflections on Religious Experience. David L. Scheidt, trans. Philadelphia: Fortress Press, 1978.

Choosing Life. Margaret Kohl, trans. Philadelphia: Fortress Press; London: SCM Press, 1981.

Of War and Love. Rita and Robert Kimber, trans. Maryknoll: Orbis Books, 1983.

The Arms Race Kills Even without War. Gerhard A. Elston, trans. Philadelphia: Fortress Press, 1983.

The Strength of the Weak: Toward a Christian Feminist Identity. Rita and Robert Kimber, trans. Philadelphia: Westminster Press, 1984.

To Work and to Love: A Theology of Creation. Shirley Cloyes, co-author. Philadelphia: Fortress Press, 1984.

Not Just Yes and Amen: Christians with a Cause. Fulbert Steffensky, co-author. Philadelphia: Fortress Press, 1985.

Hope for Faith: A Conversation. C. F. Beyers Naude, co-author. Geneva: World Council of Churches; Grand Rapids: Wm. B. Eerdmans Publishing Co., 1986.

The Window of Vulnerability: A Political Spirituality. Linda M. Maloney, trans. Minneapolis: Fortress Press, 1990.

Thinking about God: An Introduction to Theology. John Bowden, trans. Philadelphia: Trinity Press International; London: SCM Press, 1990.

Stations of the Cross: A Latin American Pilgrimage. Joyce L. Irwin, trans. Minneapolis: Fortress Press; London: Mowbray, 1993.

On Earth as in Heaven: A Liberation Spirituality of Sharing. Marc Batko, trans. Louisville: Westminster/John Knox Press, 1993.

Theology for Skeptics: Reflections on God. Joyce L. Irwin, trans. Minneapolis: Fortress Press, 1995.

Creative Disobedience. Cleveland: Pilgrim Press, 1995. (Reprint of *Beyond Mere Obedience: Reflections on a Christian Ethic for the Future*)

Mysticism and Resistance: Thou Silent Cry. Barbara and Martin Rumscheidt, trans. Minneapolis: Fortress Press, forthcoming.